ACPL ITEM
DISCARDED

Y0-BSM-576

# ALKEMA'S
## Complete Guide to
# CREATIVE ART

# for
# YOUNG
# PEOPLE

Photographs by the Author

**CHESTER JAY ALKEMA**
Assistant Professor of Art
Grand Valley State College
Allendale, Michigan

**STERLING PUBLISHING CO., INC.** NEW YORK  *Oak Tree Press Co., Ltd* London & Sydney

# OTHER BOOKS BY PROFESSOR ALKEMA

Creative Paper Crafts in Color
Complete Crayon Book
Masks
Puppet-Making

## OTHER ART BOOKS

Abstract Art
Acrylic and Other Water-Base Paints
Bridgman's Complete Guide to
    Drawing from Life
Carlson's Guide to Landscape
    Painting
Ceramics—and How to Decorate
    Them
Color in Oil Painting
Composition in Art
Constructive Anatomy
Designs—And How to Use Them

Drawing from Nature
Etching (and Other Intaglio
    Techniques)
Express Yourself in Drawing
How to Attract Attention with
    Your Art
Ikebana (Japanese Flower Arranging)
    Simplified
Joy of Drawing
Landscape Drawing with Pencil
Learn Art in One Year

Original Creations With Papier Mâché
Painting Abstract Landscapes
Painting the Sea
Postercraft
Practical Encyclopedia of Crafts
Prints—from Linoblocks
Screen Printing
Sculpture for Beginners
Stained Glass Crafting
Techniques of Drawing
Watercolor Painting for the
    Beginner

*All photographs by the author
except where indicated otherwise.*

Published in the United States of America by Sterling Publishing Co., Inc., 419 Park Avenue South, New York, N.Y. 10016

Published in 1971 in the British Commonwealth by The Oak Tree Press, Ltd., Nassau, Bahamas

Published in Australia by The Oak Tree Press Company, Ltd., P.O. Box 34, Sydney, N.S.W. 2000

Distributed in Canada by Saunders of Toronto, Ltd., Don Mills, Ontario

Distributed in United Kingdom and balance of the British Commonwealth by Ward Lock, Ltd., 116 Baker St., London, W.1

*Manufactured in Hong Kong*

Library of Congress Catalog Card No.: 70 167654
ISBN 0-8069-5188 5          UK 7061 2329 8
    5189 3

# CONTENTS

Illus. 1. You might never have seen a cat like this imaginative creature. But that's because you don't see things the same way as the third-grade artist does! Nor have you experienced the same things, such as stroking this cat's fur which he has expressed in the long lines of paint.

# CHAPTER ONE

# Creativity Is Your Aim

Ask three children to draw a cat. Do not say any more. Each child will draw upon his own experience in the creation of his cat. One might create a small, pencil-drawn, stick kitten; another, a great colorful jungle beast. The third might paint his own family cat. Look at Illus. 1 through Illus. 3. Here are three fine examples of freedom of expression. No one drew an adult's conception of a simple cat shape. Supposing you had instructed these youngsters by drawing a big ball with another, smaller, ball on top of it, two ears, a long tail, and told them to copy it. You would have had three rather poor imitations of *your* idea.

In Illus. 1, the young artist shows how impressed he is with a cat's bristly fur. The long wavy lines of paint clearly reflect his tactile experience with his pet—stroking its fur. He is obviously fascinated by the cat's tail which he has made very wide and long. The patterns, colors, and imaginative detail indicate how this cat relates to its creator's experiences, observations, and feelings.

Illus. 2 shows a far different approach. This youngster views his cat as an alert, staring creature who takes delicate careful steps. His experience with cats is obviously one of observation and admiration for the primitive, hunterlike qualities of the cat—not the cuddly softness of a pampered pet. His cat is pussyfooting through rustly leaves and is startled at every sound.

The child who created Illus. 3 has portrayed a self-image in her work. Carefully, lovingly, she holds her little kitten, indicating the strong emotional bond between child and animal. Her love for her pet canary is indicated by the prominent position of the bird cage. It also shows that the traditional enemies—cat and bird—

**Illus. 2. A completely different cat done by a tenth-grader. Who ever saw a blue cat? This artist sees the cat as an exotic animal and has expressed his impressions by using unconventional colors and shapes which immediately convey his ideas.**

**Illus. 3. Still another conception of a cat! This time it is a small warm bundle to be loved. This crayon drawing leaves no doubt its creator is a nature lover.**

They *do* see and feel things differently. In our three examples, the artists were drawing upon experience; they were motivated by their experience to express themselves. Exaggerations of form, emphasized proportions, skylines, baselines (Illus. 4) and other childlike characteristics in art—all represent truthful statements based on the

**Illus. 4. Exaggerations of form is a means of expressing ideas and impressions. This first-grader interprets the sky as a narrow blue line at the top of the painting indicating that the sky is far above her.**

live in peace and harmony in her home. This child's awareness of nature is shown also in the importance given the tree in the window and the presence of flowers in the house.

These three examples reveal that the creative approach allows each child to express himself in his own unique way. Children's standards are not the same as adults'.

it as Mommy because he *conceived* it to be her. It was the thought growing out of his experience that is important. The actual rendering at this stage is not.

It is very important that a toddler is not inhibited from making random strokes and scribbles. Very often parents or other adults grab the pencil from a 2- or 3-year-old (see Illus. 5) and say, "That's not how you make a person, Johnny. Here, let me show you." Anyone who has observed this situation knows that Johnny watches

Illus. 5. "Mommy" as created by a 3-year-old. His intent was to paint a picture of her, and if the result is not immediately recognizable, it is no less a valid portrait than a photographic image would be.

children's own personal lives. The realities of children are just as valid as the realities of adults. Let us look at Illus. 5 through Illus. 9.

The center of the universe of small children is "Mommy." She is the first contact and experience with the world that they have. Therefore, when children first start their scribblings, you will often find a great blob or cometlike lines that a 3-year-old will hold up proudly and announce, "This is Mommy!" And it *is* Mommy. He sees

Illus. 6. "Mommy" has started to take shape in the hands of a 4½-year-old, who has graphically depicted "Mommy Going to the Hospital to Get a Baby."

7

momentarily and wanders away. Johnny knows perfectly well that he is not capable of rendering such perfect circles and lines. He is more than likely hurt and confused that his efforts were "wrong." By the age of $4\frac{1}{2}$, an average child has developed the motor control to depict a "Mommy" more recognizable to the adult. Illus. 6 shows a rendering of "Mommy Going to the Hospital to Get a Baby." This child's observation and awareness all led to this painting. If Mommy has no arms, it is of little matter—the artist was not concerned with Mommy's limbs at the time he set out to create his image of her.

Illus. 7 shows a kindergarten child's conception of Mommy. By this stage, emotion has entered the picture— Mommy is smiling and therefore happy. This painting symbolizes the child's experience of receiving love and affection from her mother. She is looking straight ahead and her smile is directed toward her.

By the time a child has reached the fourth grade, his

Illus. 7. "Mommy" is here rendered by a kindergartener in the typical geometric fashion for his age—a circle for the head and vertical lines for the body. Legs and arms will appear later, but the important thing the artist is expressing is apparent—Mommy is happy.

Illus. 8. A fourth-grader is able to show his deep emotional feeling for his home in "My Family." Here are three things he loves—his mother, his baby brother and his bicycle.

Illus. 9. Creative art contributes greatly to the mental, emotional and motor development of children. This seventh-grade artist recreated a very important day in his family life—"The Day Our Family Had Pups." Such experiences are of intense interest and concern to youngsters.

experience has grown as well as his ability to express himself in terms easily understood by the adult world. Illus. 8 shows a fourth-grade boy's warm feeling for the home he loves. The things dear to him—his mother, his baby brother, his bicycle—convey the richness of his home environment.

The whole family, the house, the locale, and his pets have developed out of a seventh-grader's personal experience in Illus. 9. This painting commemorates a very special day in his life when the family dog had pups. The event could have happened some time previous to the rendering of it, but the impressions are so strong that not a detail is forgotten.

Creative expressions do not all relate to pleasure, however. Fears play an important role in childhood and adolescence. Very often, children in calling upon

their own experience, express their conflicts and fears in art—a healthy outlet. Many children as well as adults cannot put fears into words—more often than not they are even unconscious of them. However, one of the important solutions to overcoming fear is to express it.

In Illus. 10, a child relives her experience of being chased by a dog. This is a very interesting painting because it symbolizes the little girl's striving to overcome her fear. Certainly, in her dreams the dog was a great evil monster and she was small and incapable of coping with the menace. However, when she put her idea down on paper, she made herself enormous and the dog became a tiny, ineffectual creature. She no doubt placed the whole situation in perspective in her mind and the next time she encountered her foe she probably was better able to deal with him.

Illus. 10. "The Dog Is Chasing Me." Here a second-grader depicts one of the most common fears of childhood, that of being chased and bitten by animals. Notice how the "ferocious" dog has shrunk into rather insignificant proportions. Although she is crying "help," she has obviously already helped herself by expressing her bad experience.

Illus. 11. A painful ordeal is relived by a third-grader in "A Visit to the Dentist."

Another common dread in childhood (and one that extends often into adulthood) is "A Visit to the Dentist" (Illus. 11). This third-grade boy, through his painting, bravely faces the drill again. However, by viewing this painful encounter as an onlooker and not from the dentist's chair, he finds that it really wasn't so terrible. He sees the dentist as a perfectly ordinary person and not a looming ogre peering down his throat. The nurse is a bustling, pleasant-looking lady, and the entire office is quite cheerful. These good impressions actually overcame the bad impression of pain because they are what the boy is expressing in his artwork.

Another example of this can be seen in Illus. 12. This fifth-grade artist depicts himself as being unusually small on the operating table, which is a means of expressing how helpless he felt. Nonetheless, through all the terror of the environment, he retained vivid images of the people and details such as the clock on the wall, indicating the time of the great event.

In early childhood, perhaps the most universal fear is that of the dark. A kindergarten girl reveals in her painting, "Walking at Night" (Illus. 13), how she feels when she is surrounded by blackness. However, she is trying to resolve her fears by bringing them out in the open, whether she is conscious of it or not.

Art can also be a means whereby a child can hide, or sublimate, his feelings of hate or spiteful acts of aggression. A certain fifth-grader was generally disliked by his class members. He picked on younger children and avoided his contemporaries. He went out of his way to irritate his teacher and ignored reprimands. He did, however, enjoy all of the attention he received as a

Illus. 12. In "My Operation," you might have to strain to locate the tiny patient who happens to be a big fifth-grader. However, he has shown himself as being almost baby-size. Either he was wishing he could shrivel up into nothing at the time or he did indeed feel very small and helpless.

11

renegade. This boy was talented in art, and in a class project produced a beautiful woven article which his teacher praised highly and hung in the main hallway of the school. He was amazed at the attention he received, and it taught him a valuable lesson—so much so that it was a turning point in his conduct. He learned that recognition comes more easily as the result of a constructive act and that his pleasure was much greater than when he had acted badly. His art developed as his attitudes changed and his experience widened.

As you can see, creative art experiences encourage a child to be individual and original in expressing ideas. They cause the child to make discoveries, to experiment, to make "mistakes." The child comes to believe that it is his ideas that are wanted above all else. He is drawing upon his own world, limited as it might be in adult eyes. Instead of being told, "Do this, do that,"—like the game, "Simon Says"—he is free to do what *he* wants and is capable of doing.

By allowing children to develop their own creativity in art you will soon find that with a minimum of guidance they will work out orderly habits in drawing and painting. By experience they will learn that it is best to put in big broad areas of sky first, with foreground objects on top of the blue. Intuitively, children will plan and work so that lines, shapes, colors, and textures are organized, orderly and logical. In addition, creative art experiences open up avenues to materials and tools that are best suited to the ideas children are trying to express. At the same time, a child's ability to co-ordinate eye and hand movements improves. Improved muscular control allows a child to master more complicated techniques so that he can best achieve his desired effects. As painting, drawing, pasting, tearing, and cutting activities increase, the child will learn to pick and choose the medium most suitable for his creations.

There are many ways of selecting stimulating topics to inspire young people to express themselves as you will soon see. The important thing to bear in mind is that probably not more than one in thirty children will assume the role of an adult, practicing artist. The purpose of this book is not to train children to become skilled artists in the fullest sense of the word. Rather, it is to allow each child to respond to his environment

Illus. 13. "Walking at Night" is an example of how one little kindergartener was able to tell how she feels in the dark. Surrounded by black she squarely faces the thing that frightens her the most dressed from head to toe in bright, cheerful colors.

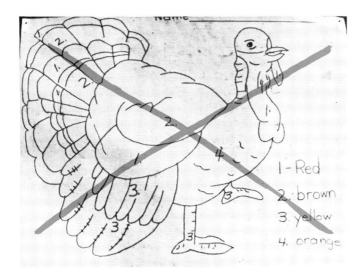

**Illus. 14. Can you imagine what the title of this might be? Perhaps, "I Will Fill in the Outline Exactly as Told"!**

**Illus. 15. "I Am Happy Today." Could this kindergarten child have said that about Illus. 14?**

and to draw upon his experiences in his own childlike way. The expression of an idea is far more important to a child's development than the acquisition of specific art skills.

Can you imagine two more disparate paintings than Illus. 14 and Illus. 15? If a child filled in the turkey color by color, could he label the finished product "I Am Happy Today"? Would it say anything about *him*? The artist who painted Illus. 15 was part of a group of kindergarten students who might have been told by the teacher, "Suppose I ask you how you feel today. Could you draw your answer for me?" Surely the filled-in turkey expresses nothing whatever—except perhaps an hour's wasted time!

The main part of this book is devoted to presenting topics and ideas that motivate children in art. Another large part offers ideas for exploring various media which provide rewarding avenues for self-expression. Right now, in the next chapter, let us explore some of the means by which you can choose and present topics and procedures for motivating children in art.

CHAPTER TWO

# Setting the Stage

As you now know, a child's artwork is the direct result of his experience—whether environmental, mental or emotional. One of the vital roles that you as an adult can play is affording a child as many creative art experiences as you possibly can. Small children have far less control over widening their horizons than do older, more independent, children. Remember always that the creative spark is waiting to be kindled. Try to be alert to things that catch a child's interest or attention.

The creative art experience does not happen in a vacuum. You set the stage and a child will take it from there.

In Illus. 16, three children have been allowed to bring a tiny baby bird into their home. Perhaps it had fallen from its nest and been found by the children. The two toddlers have never seen a baby bird before and their interest and wonder is obvious. At this point, it is a good idea to set out the children's art supplies—crayons, pencils, construction paper, collage materials, scissors or whatever they are capable of using and suggest that they might like to show how they feel about the little newcomer. The big brother who may or may not have been acquainted with an infant bird is enriching his own experience by observing the smaller children's reactions and acting as guardian for the little orphan.

Illus. 16. Would you recognize the importance of such an experience as holding and feeding a baby bird as a source of creative art? For young children who cannot yet put their feelings into words, art is the ideal outlet. (Photo courtesy of "Grand Rapids Press.")

**Illus. 17. "Bird Watching" reveals the result of an actual episode—that of holding a bird —in the life of a first-grader.**

Illus. 17 shows the result of this everyday kind of incident. This is not the kind of painting that would have been created without stimulation. Holding a bird in one's hand is not an experience every child enjoys. Having actually felt the creature, fed it, stroked it and comforted it, brings a great reality to the painting. Allow children to pick up worms, walk in mud, climb trees, and you enlarge their world in every sense—touch, sound, sight and smell.

When a small child squeezes his cereal through his fingers and examines the results like a research scientist, he has increased his knowledge enormously—difficult though this is to imagine for an adult who views such activity from quite a different viewpoint ("Oh, no!"). The day a child first walks to school alone, he begins to see things along the route that he had never noticed before. When a youngster attends an early evening film for the first time, the whole world looks different to him. His awareness is far more acute and his experience grows in leaps and bounds. These are all important in fostering creative art. Encourage a child to express these experiences in paint or whatever medium he wishes. Children are like sponges—absorbing to the point of bursting and unable to communicate their feelings verbally. This is why art is of such great value as a means of expression for the young and why children's art so often has great beauty and intensity of feeling.

Since games and play are constant and never-ending activities, you might suggest a very broad topic in this way. "Summer is coming soon. Would you like to tell me the game that you most enjoy playing with your friends?" In this way you are providing the idea in a general way although you have pinpointed the topic sufficiently so that the child immediately conjures up

15

**Illus. 18.** "Playing Hopscotch with my Friend" is recalled here by a second-grader as a pleasurable summer pastime.

images of summers past and the fun he had. He is eager to express how much he is looking forward to certain pleasurable experiences. In Illus. 18, a second-grader portrays himself and his friend and his cat playing hopscotch in front of his house. Another child, in the third grade, recalls the joy of flying kites with his best friends in Illus. 19. The fourth-grader who painted the relay race in Illus. 20 is expressing his growing interest in group games and competitive sports. Perhaps he attended a camp for the first time and is depicting an important race that he

**Illus. 19.** Another youngster's happiest memory of his summer days is shown in "We Are Flying Our Kites." Such seemingly simple activities are excellent sources for genuinely creative art. Notice the freedom with which this child painted his scene, indicating the enthusiasm which he felt for the subject.

Illus. 20. A meaningful event in the life of one fourth-grader is depicted in "The Relay Race." Did he win? Lose? Was it his first relay race? For some reason, it stands out in his mind, and that is what matters.

participated in and was on the winning team. Although he may have reported this great event to his family, the special significance of the experience may never have been realized.

Another fourth-grader expresses a different kind of summer activity that obviously has great meaning for him in "My Dad and I Go Fishing and Camping" (Illus. 21). His experience camping out with his father overshadows all of his other previous summer activities at the moment. Such an expression of his feelings could come as a great surprise to the parent involved who may have wondered if his son had been lonely without his friends and had made up his mind to wait a few more years before repeating the venture. Again, this could be an example of how vital art can be as a means for children to express a deep emotion.

Any season of the year provides a good starting point as a motivational topic. "What I Like Best to Do in Winter" could be divided into inside and outside activities,

since winter is a long spell and encompasses a wide range of subjects. The first snowfall is always a joyful event and is a perfect starting point for "Fun in the Snow." This broad topic provides each child with an opportunity to express the activity he likes best. If, however, you were to suggest "Sliding in the Snow," you would be giving them a narrow, assigned topic. There would be little spontaneity and the subject might have no meaning for the children who either have no sleds or are not interested in sliding. These children would have to strain their imaginations to depict an experience that does not exist for them.

There is always danger that an assigned topic will bypass the interest and desires of some children. An assigned topic is most effective when it relates to experiences a child has had or that are common to a group of children. For instance, a visit to a firehouse by several children would provide a common experience but each child would respond to the topic in his own way.

Illus. 21. Experiences shared by children with their parents provide excellent sources for artwork. Although children often tend to pretend indifference as far as family activities are concerned, "My Dad and I Go Fishing and Camping" proves otherwise.

On the other hand, look at Illus. 22 through Illus. 25. The fourth-grader who painted "Playing in the Snow" has included an abundance of jolly activities that are very meaningful to him. He loves to make snowmen, to toboggan, ski and slide, and just generally to romp in the snow, while the young second-grader in Illus. 23 obviously prefers "Sliding" above all else. Perhaps a brand-new flying saucer is responsible for her enthusiasm. "Skiing is the Most Fun" is the title a third-grade boy gave his artwork (Illus. 25). All of these children are depicting personally meaningful experiences. They were able to relate to the more general topic of "Fun in the Snow."

Illus. 23. "Sliding" is the snow fun most enjoyed by this youngster who is riding on a flying saucer.

18

Illus. 24. "Whee-ee" is the title of a third-grader's painting of himself and his friend ice-skating. There is no question what he likes best to do in winter.

Illus. 25. Another third-grader thinks "Skiing is the Most Fun."

19

Illus. 26. The topic "School Sports" inspired a fourth-grader to depict himself performing gymnastics which he has entitled "Doing Stunts." He appears to have a rubber-band quality which is undoubtedly the way he feels when performing.

Illus. 27. "Ice Hockey" shows an important moment when the goalie foiled a score attempt as indicated by the cheering "Wings."

Illus. 28. Another thrilling moment in sports history is captured in "The Baseball Game," showing the runner hitting base seconds before the ball entered the mitt.

One sixth-grade teacher decided to motivate her students to portray the various Olympic Games that were taking place in a foreign country. She discussed the sports events with the class—explained what the discus throw was, the javelin, the shot put, etc. The class haltingly set to work without enthusiasm and produced halfhearted, unimaginative paintings and drawings. Obviously the Olympics were as far away as the moon and the children had no direct knowledge of them. Fortunately, she had the insight to recognize her mistake and switched the subject to "School Sports." There was no hesitation this time. All the students set to work and showed their favorite gym or extracurricular sport. First-hand experiences must be considered if art expression is to be meaningful.

Examples of the kinds of things they might have shown can be seen in Illus. 26 through Illus. 30, although these were all done by students in various grades. They all have a high degree of reality and they are rich in detail and have "life." Why? Because the young artists all are depicting activities they have observed or performed.

Illus. 29. In the mind of one seventh-grader "Girls' Basketball" stands out as the most interesting school sport. She has gone to considerable pains to render all of the members of her gym class. Notice the one large figure who is the only one facing front, and probably represents the artist herself.

Illus. 30. Another seventh-grader finds "Ice Skating" the joy of his life. Whether he is really this accomplished or not, it is how he sees himself. He has managed successfully to convey the twirling movement of this kind of skating by giving the arena a wheel-like effect.

**Illus. 31.** Everyday experiences associated with school life provide numerous topics for expression in art. Here a fifth-grader portrays a teacher who probably means a great deal to him. Although she undoubtedly makes school life enjoyable for him, he has, nonetheless, set the clock at 3:00, indicating the end of the school day!

Motivational art topics must relate to the interests of children at each stage in their development. Watch children in the playground, backyard or playroom and take note of the various activities and interests they are pursuing. Observe how these activities change from season to season, from sunny day to cloudy day. Discuss these activities with a child and you will inspire him to recapture the magic moments of his daily life.

Children's interests exist in both the world of reality and the world of make-believe; therefore, motivational art topics should allow children to remain inventive in their thinking. You might be tempted to *over-motivate*—that is, to press the subject too hard by going into great detail or by probing to the point of causing confusion in a child's mind. If you simply initiate a discussion, you will soon find that a child's imagination and enthusiasm will take over. And this is the time to get started in the act of creating. By channelling the excitement of the moment into active painting, drawing, modelling or other media, you provide the means for the child to create at his best. Over-long discussions cause children to lose interest.

It is always well to have art materials at hand prior to the motivational discussion. The perfect psychological moment could be lost if the children have to wait. An example of the importance of this occurred once when a student teacher who was giving art lessons to a group of third- and fourth-grade youngsters brought her puppy into class. She had planned a lengthy discussion of what he did, what he ate, where he slept, all the funny little things he did, in an attempt to provide ideas for the children to paint. As she began, she was amazed to see all the students starting to paint. The presence of the live puppy already up to his tricks inspired them immediately and there was really nothing to be said. They expressed *their* ideas—not the teacher's!

Not all such art-provoking situations happen this easily. In most cases, you will have to set the ball rolling yourself after the topic is presented by asking certain pertinent questions. Relating to the broad or the narrow topic, the questions might revolve around the general queries "What?" "Where?" "Who?" "How?" If the broad topic "Fun in the Snow" is discussed, first establish the action by asking questions beginning with "What?" "*What* games do you enjoy playing in the snow?"

Illus. 32. An exciting event in any school is "Fire Drill," here painted by a third-grader. That she enjoys it is evident by the smiling faces on everyone, including the teacher, who is obviously pleased by the orderly group in her charge.

Next, enrich the child's mental image of the action's environment by asking, "*Where* do you play your game? Many of you like to slide in the snow. Where do you slide? Is there a hill there? A fence? Trees? Pond? Describe the scene." Then determine the people involved in the chosen activity by asking "*Who* is performing the game? You? Your friends? Parents? Describe these people. What are they wearing on such a cold day? Describe the patterns you might wish to add to their coats, scarves, snow pants—patterns such as polka dots, stripes, checkerboards, etc."

Finally, ask questions beginning with "How?" When possible, have body demonstrations of the activity. If many children mention sliding, strengthen their identification with action by having a child demonstrate the position of the body when sliding down hill. "How do you slide down a hill? Show me." Ask further questions designed to show that the head is held up to view the path ahead. The legs bend at the knee causing the sled to swerve off course. The arms and hands are held forward, clutching the steering apparatus. In addition to viewing the model, ask children to assume the same body position as the model to actually feel the action of the body in performing the activity.

Now that you have learned what "Setting the Stage" for creative art activities means, let us proceed in the following chapters to explore some of the specific *ways* in which you as a parent or teacher can actually provide meaningful experiences for your children. Although we will discuss a great variety of motivational topics, there are many, many more that you will undoubtedly come up with as you develop your awareness of creative art experiences.

# CHAPTER THREE

# Excursions

**Illus. 33. The author takes the children for a "looking walk" to investigate the various kinds of houses in town. Although the children had often passed these houses they were amazed to discover all the things they had never noticed before. The drawings they made before and after show the results of this enriching excursion.**

An excursion can be as simple as going into the garage, into a flower garden or visiting a bakery. The world is so full of details that we often see things without *really* seeing them. We have impressions of our daily environment, but if called upon to describe in detail a certain tree in the backyard, the result would be sketchy.

The fourth-graders who produced the pictures of the houses on these pages were first called upon by their teacher simply to draw a picture of a house and to color all areas of their papers. This was the only instruction given. She did not attempt to motivate or guide them as they worked. This was an experiment I chose to make in a school which did not have a regular art program. My objective in conducting the experiment was to determine the extent to which details in children's artwork might be enriched when a teacher effectively motivates

children. How might a child's art product change when you first ask him to draw a house—and later you motivate him to become consciously aware of many details relating to a house?

A week after this, I visited the classroom and conducted a follow-up activity. I told the boys and girls we were going to draw a house, but first we were going to take a "looking walk" down one block in town. The children often walked down this block on the way to school and were undoubtedly familiar in a general way with the houses. But they had never stood in front of any house and studied it.

First we observed the different kinds of windows each house had. I asked questions to help them see that some windows were square, others rectangular, and one house actually had an octagonal-shaped window! Some

Illus. 34. Here is a startling example of the effect of the looking walk which obviously did a great deal to stir Tracy's imagination. The pattern of the breezeway on the left is quite unlike anything seen on the excursion, nor were there any kites in evidence. Her house has undergone a transformation in the form of different kinds of windows, shingling and an ornamental door and house number.

Illus. 35A. Before

Illus. 35B. After

Illus. 35. Bryan's first house is a typical plain little saltbox with a minimum of detail. However, his second house is a forceful, bright rendering of the same basic shape. He has added an ornamental brick pattern, a house number, chimney, steps. The bare areas surrounding the house now contain a picket fence, garage, and tree. He has filled in all areas of his composition.

Illus. 36. Vickie's house has undergone drastic alterations. A wealth of detail has been added—even a figure in one of the windows. Her entire drawing is more boldly executed, and although most of the children stuck to the same basic colors, Vickie's colors are entirely different.

Illus. 36A. Before

Illus. 36B. After

**Illus. 37A. Before**

**Illus. 37B. After**

**Illus. 37.** Again, a considerable change has taken place, this time in Charles' houses. His second house is a completely different shape, and the entire house is adorned with patterns and different colors. The environment surrounding the house has become a maze of objects—fences, flowers, a tree, a swing set, a television tower, and even a cat has entered the picture!

**Illus. 38.** Michele's house shows major changes, although in both examples she reveals an understanding of perspective unusual for a fourth-grader. Notice that she has retained the same colors, but has changed her concept of almost everything else—shapes, objects, etc., as well as filling the entire paper with her composition.

**Illus. 38A. Before**

**Illus. 38B. After**

Illus. 39. Wayne's house, top, created before the "looking walk" and discussion, shows a plain unpatterned surface. The colors are solid, the trimming held to a minimum. In his "After" house, the shape is similar, but there are strong differences. A garage and breezeway have been added, shingle patterns on the roofs and other designs on the rest of the house. Little details such as a mailbox and house number have also been added.

Illus. 39B. After

**Illus. 40A. Before**

Illus. 40. Sherrie's house has undergone no change as far as its shape is concerned. However, her awareness of detail has increased enormously. Her plain green roof has shingles, her trees have grown considerably and her entire rendering is bolder and more assured. She now knows her subject!

**Illus. 40B. After**

Illus. 41. On-the-spot drawing and painting is very exciting and beneficial for older children. "Skyline" painted by a tenth-grader portrays an impressionistic view of a city.

window panes were separated by wood strips, some ran horizontally, some vertically; some were spaced close together, some far apart, creating a variety of patterns and designs. Some windows had curtains; others had shades; still others had blinds; some had shutters; a few had windowboxes. There were a number of different kinds of awnings—metal, canvas, solid-colored, striped.

Then we focussed on the porches. These varied as much as the windows—small, large, covered, uncovered, closed in, open, with railings, without railings. I asked the children if they noticed differences in the roofs of the houses. First they discussed the differences in color, then the materials, textures, and patterns. We saw how the roofs had different slopes, some had peaks, dormers, attic windows, chimneys. Even the television antennae

varied—one antenna was supported by a tall, complicated tower (Illus. 37B).

Particularly interesting were the diverse patterns produced by the sidings. Some houses were made of brick, others of wood siding or shingles. The lines varied accordingly. Even garages were unique. One garage had a breezeway, another a basketball net. Doors either went up or opened out.

After examining the structures themselves, we looked at all the things surrounding each house. The children started describing shrubs, flower beds, open-air fireplaces, swing sets, bird baths, fences, picnic tables, sidewalks, driveways, street signs, street lights, and a multitude of different environmental objects. When I saw that the boys and girls were really excited about what they were "seeing" for the first time, we returned to the classroom and they began drawing immediately. I walked around the room making observations that everyone could hear, such as: "Look, John put a mailbox in front of his house"; "Jane remembered the house number"; Mark put in the octagonal window." This not only pleased the individual artists but encouraged the others to recall the details of the excursion.

Now, compare the finished crayon drawings (marked "B") with the first set (marked "A") made before the excursion!

With younger children such as these fourth-graders, all the art activities relating to the excursion should take place in the home or classroom. On-the-spot drawing or painting tends to confuse the young child—he is likely to be overwhelmed by the abundant detail and to find it difficult to be selective. In addition, the mere burden of carrying art supplies and working under out-of-doors conditions is harder for a youngster—he tends to drop things, or accidentally tear his paper, or be distracted by activities going on in the area.

On the other hand, older boys and girls benefit greatly from "working from nature" as Illus. 41 through Illus. 44 show. With these youngsters you can be a little more general in your discussion of the scene they choose to draw. Probably the best first question would be, "What do you think is the most important or most interesting thing you see?" Once the youngsters have a focal point —a center of interest located off center—they will be able to work around it in all directions, adding detail.

An excursion allows children to gain deeper insights and awareness of the workings of their community. At the same time, you will be able to see how much a child gained from the experience. His artwork will tell you what he enjoyed most as well as his ability to understand new ideas he was exposed to. In a sense, art serves as a window which allows you to view the impressions and emotions of a child.

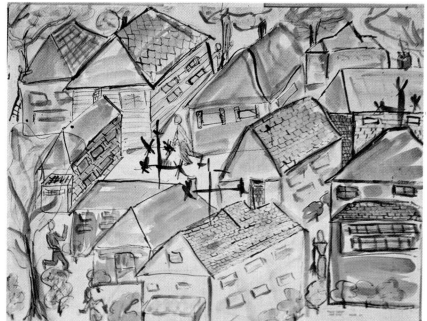

**Illus. 42. "Back Yards"** is another example of the ability of older youngsters to handle an on-the-spot art session. This twelfth-grader has effectively captured an intimate view from a high vantage point. His composition extends to and beyond the paper, giving life and reality to the work.

Illus. 43. "The Free Methodist Church on Maple Street" is rendered in an almost architectural, but nonetheless free, manner by a ninth-grader in white India ink on black paper.

Illus. 44. A sixth-grader depicts "A House on Portage Street" during an out-of-doors drawing excursion. Notice that at this age the young artist tends to be more detailed and graphic in his representation than the older students in Illus. 41, 42, and 43.

**Illus. 45.** Following an enlightening bus tour through their own city, a second-grade class undertook to create a mural showing "**Our City Helpers.**" Everyone worked on it and contributed ideas, so that hardly a detail of the excursion was forgotten. Notice that the people—the workmen, milkman, policeman, nurses—overshadow the colored chalk background of buildings, vehicles, etc.

A fascinating "trip" is a bus ride through your city. The colorful, bustling mural in Illus. 45 is the result of an interesting bus excursion a group of second-graders took through the business and residential district of their city. The children were eager to see all of the areas they had never visited before as well as to get acquainted with all the different people who play a part in city life—policemen, milkmen, mailmen, garbage men, etc. During the excursion, questions were asked to bring their attention to activities, people and buildings: "What buildings do you see on this street? Can you name them? What are the shapes of the buildings? Tall, short, wide, thin? Are they colored? Dull?

The children decided they would all get together and put their impressions down in a big mural. They used colored chalk to depict the buildings and background detail. Scrap materials—leather, cloth, metallic papers, construction paper, tagboard and wallpaper were used to make the figures which were glued to the background.

You might suggest to older children that a mural would be a fine way if showing the life history of a loaf of bread. They could visit a large bakery and see men and machines at work. Their mural could trace the steps the bread goes through, right from its beginnings in the wheat field to the packaged loaf. Or a visit to the post office might result in the story of one letter.

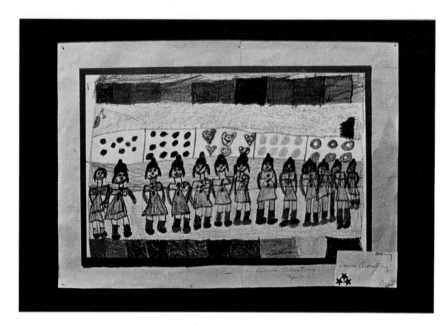

Illus. 46. "The Bakery," as drawn by one Brownie after her troop visited various places in the city in preparation for a national art competition. All of the Brownies were in the second grade. This little girl gave equal attention to the Brownies and the baked goods.

The Brownies of Wyoming, Michigan, wanted to enter a national competition to portray their local community in art. The Brownie leaders took their troops to many local places, such as the firehouse, a nearby bakery, and the community water tower. The first stop was the bakery. Illus. 46 and Illus. 47 both show very happy scenes, but these two Brownie artists produced very different pictures. Illus. 46 shows the whole group in the bakery. The scene is from the standpoint of the way the Brownies and their leader looked in the bakery to the clerk. Then, in Illus. 47, we see how the clerk and the bakery looked to the Brownies. Each of these little girls saw the very same thing but each had a different viewpoint and impression. Because their leader did not tell them *what* to draw, the girls brought their individual expressions to their artwork. Had they not been taken to the bakery but told to draw the inside of a bakery, would they have produced such interesting details as the clock on the wall, the picture, the different shapes and colors of the cookies on the shelves?

Illus. 47. Another Brownie in her impression of "The Bakery" shows a greater concern for the baked goods and the interior of the shop.

34

Illus. 48. The next stop for the Brownies was the local firehouse. Naturally, the most impressive thing to everyone was the fire engine. This Brownie has remembered the engine in realistic detail.

Illus. 50. The last stop for the troop was the town water tower. Compare this painting with Illus. 51. You would scarcely believe it was the same tower!

Illus. 49. Another Brownie has made a quick impression of the fire engine. She went away with powerful images of colors and shapes.

Illus. 51. As you can see from comparing this with Illus. 50, these two Brownies were not copying what they saw—rather they were reproducing their own images in their own way. This is creative expression in art.

**Illus. 52. A tenth-grade's excursion led to this painting of "The Farmer's Market," a vividly executed piece of art revealing a great awareness of people, as well as objects.**

From the bakery the Brownies proceeded to the firehouse. Although they had a thorough tour of the firehouse and all its equipment and met the firemen, almost all of the children drew one image that impressed them the most—the big, shiny fire engine. Illus. 48 and Illus. 49 show a representational rendering and an abstract one. The child who painted Illus. 48 had a vivid picture in her mind of the red engine and the time she was looking at it, as indicated by the clock. On the other hand, the abstract artist's head was full of colorful impressions which she rendered in various shapes and relationships.

The last stop was the town water tower. Here again you can see how differently two Brownies saw the same subject (Illus. 50 and Illus. 51). Neither one of them copied the water tower exactly. It doesn't matter that the tree has moved from one side to the other. Actually, this freedom to interpret is exactly the kind of thing that you should encourage in a child instead of saying, "Joan, the tree is in the *wrong* place!" Look at Betty's painting— she has done it *right*." Nothing could confuse Joan more than being told, not that her painting is wrong, but that she *saw* the scene incorrectly, since her art is an expression of her own response to it.

36

Illus. 53. In the painting, "Monotony of Labor," a twelfth-grader realistically conveys his impressions of a visit to a local factory.

Illus. 54. A wealth of material can be gathered for creative art by a visit to "The Zoo." This crayon drawing was done by a third-grader who appears to have been impressed by two things—the lion and the sign "Don't Feed the Animals." However, even though he is depicting the zoo, the main focus seems to be upon the people he saw there. Count them—there are 10 humans and only one animal! (The dog doesn't count.)

Illus. 55. A trip to visit a working farm is an exciting adventure for town and city children. The farmer is showing this group a piece of farm equipment which they are allowed to touch.
(Photo courtesy of Edith Brockway and "Arts and Activities.")

For city children, almost no excursion is as much fun as a trip to a farm. "Riding" on a tractor or holding a baby pig, stroking a horse, watching cows at milking time—all are rare and exciting events for children who do not live in rural areas. The memory of a farm excursion will remain in their minds for many years and enrich their experience greatly. You can just look at the happy faces of the children in the photographs and imagine the many exciting drawings and paintings they produced from this experience.

"Susie Milks a Cow" (Illus. 61) is ample proof of the

Illus. 56. A very happy boy has the experience of his life—riding on the big farm tractor. Such events as this provide rich material for creative art as you can see on the opposite page.
(Photo courtesy of Edith Brockway and "Arts and Activities.")

Illus. 57. A first-grader has rendered his colorful impressions of riding on the farm tractor in crayon. He has even included some small bystanders.

Illus. 58. A seventh-grader shows his tractor performing a different task—hauling a load of hay.

Illus. 59. For many children, touching a real horse is a once-in-a-lifetime event and not easily forgotten. A unique experience such as this can produce unique and individual expression in art.
(Photo courtesy of Edith Brockway and "Arts and Activities.")

Illus. 60. Imagine holding a baby pig in your arms! It would be difficult for these children to describe in words how they felt about it, but they would be almost certain to convey their emotions in their artwork.
(Photo courtesy of Edith Brockway and "Arts and Activities.")

Illus. 61. "Susie Milks a Cow" depicts a rare experience in the life of a first-grader.

Illus. 62. Another first-grader has shown quite a different cow, but it is obvious that the milking process is also uppermost in this artist's mind.

effect of first-hand knowledge. This first-grader has graphically reproduced the hand-milking process. The cow looks more like a camel and the chicken seems to be flying in the air, but Susie's main point is the fact that she actually milked a cow. The same holds true for the unique cow in Illus. 62 who has three legs in front and one in back! However, this little artist portrayed her subject faithfully as she saw it.

While still at the farm you can draw attention to all the different characteristics and habits each animal has. Point out sizes, colors and shapes; eating, sleeping and bathing habits; reactions to people—friendly, unfriendly; texture—soft, furry, bristly, etc. Bring these things up again before the art session to refresh the child's memory. One thing will lead to another and another. (A trip to the farm would also be a good subject for a group mural.)

**Illus. 63.** One twelfth-grade artist's fondest memories of summer revolve around the local swimming hole. Here he pictures himself and all of his friends. About to finish high school and approaching adulthood he may be feeling that this pleasurable vacation experience is about to come to an end for him.

CHAPTER FOUR

# Vacations and Travel

Vacations and travel provide excellent material for young people's artwork. You do not have to travel to the far ends of the earth to have a meaningful experience —even a family outing to a park, a trip from a small town to a big city, or camping-out are exciting adventures for children.

Since summer offers the longest period of time and the most opportunity for a variety of experiences, this is a good starting point for your initiating a discussion. For instance, if your child went to camp for two weeks, he undoubtedly would bubble over with all of the things he did and saw. You could ask him if he would like to put his impressions down in paint or crayon or even make a mural of his own showing all of the different things he liked best. If you are a teacher, the first two weeks of school is the opportune time to capture enthusiasm over summer activities or travel.

Start with the broad topic, "What I Did This Summer." The most outstanding event in the child's mind is bound to come bursting out. The broad topic could be narrowed down to a day at the beach, which in turn might result in a painting of digging a hole to China, making castles in the sand, diving off the raft, or just lying under a beach umbrella.

Another child might have taken a trip to a fascinating city, such as did the second-grader who produced Illus. 65. This child visited a large ocean port, such as New York or San Francisco. He obviously was impressed by the bridges and ocean liners that he saw—perhaps for the first time in his life! He could never have made such a

**Illus. 64. "Roasting Hot Dogs in Milham Park"** shows a fifth-grader's experience of camping out with her family, obviously a warm and meaningful memory to her.

Illus. 65. A large ocean port visited by a second-grader provided a thrilling experience. Possibly this youngster had never seen anything like this in his life. A gigantic bridge and an ocean liner are not easily forgotten. He has even included two sea gulls which might also have been completely new to him.

personal expression of this kind if he had not seen them with his own eyes. He undoubtedly saw many things in the city, but these may have related more closely to his own environment, whereas the port facilities were a whole new experience.

This is true of Illus. 66, too. This fifth-grader has reproduced a magical moment in his life—"The City at Night." The wonderful detail of the buildings and park, the intricate structure of the bridge, the starry sky, give the impression of a fairy land—which indeed it was for this child. If you had asked the boy to describe in words how he felt about the city, he could never have expressed the beauty and majesty that he was able to communicate in this painting. Supposing it had been New York City that he had visited, and you said, "Oh, Jack, draw a picture of the Empire State Building." Poor Jack might not have taken particular notice of this great landmark,

and he would have had to strain his memory to satisfy your request. But a general question such as "What was the city like, Jack?" would have immediately given Jack the opportunity to express his own images of the visit.

As well as discussing the actual place of the trip, you might ask questions about how he got there—bus, car, air, ship. A child could be strongly impressed by the fact that he was eating lunch in a plane while flying over a big river or having dinner on a train while whizzing through a major city, or brushing his teeth when the train suddenly went through a tunnel! Such experiences would produce truly individual artwork. A child who visited Mackinac Island in Michigan discovered that cars were not allowed! Can you imagine the effect of this on a youngster who lives entirely in a mechanized world? No wonder he chose to paint "Riding in a Buggy" (Illus. 67)—

Illus. 66. "The City at Night" releases an exciting image in the mind of a fifth-grader. Although his rendering is very carefully detailed, the art has a strong impressionistic quality.

he had been transported back to an age he may have seen in movies and television, but which meant little to him as far as reality was concerned.

Another unusual vehicle ride is shown in Illus. 68—the San Francisco cable car. This seventh-grader has a strong eye for detail. He not only remembered the street names on the car but the name of the little lunchroom. Notice how he placed people and interior scenes in the windows of the houses at the right. He emphasized the steep incline of the cable car with the many verticals that compose the rest of the picture. This is a good example of how children can intuitively develop a strong sense of composition and design.

Illus. 67. Where in the world can you ride in an old-fashioned buggy? On Mackinac Island, Michigan, where another fifth-grader had this rare experience, which resulted in this crayon drawing.

Illus. 68. Travel to such places as San Francisco inevitably leads to new adventures. A seventh-grader depicts "San Francisco Cable Car" in a well-balanced and interesting composition.

Illus. 69. "Carnival Time" shows a tenth-grader's vivid recollections of an enjoyable day. His activities there are all depicted—riding on the roller coaster, airplanes, and other rides, as well as winning a teddy bear, which may have been the highlight, since it is displayed prominently in the foreground.

Illus. 70. "On the Ferris Wheel" proved to be the most exciting carnival activity for a seventh-grader who depicts herself and her friends happily spinning around.

Amusement parks, carnivals, county fairs and circuses are other important sources of creative art experiences. The panorama of activities, things to do, to eat and to see, could produce a multitude of drawings and paintings as shown in Illus. 69 through 72. Illus. 73 portrays a ninth-grader's experience during a Spring vacation when his family went to New Orleans for the Mardi Gras—a gala and festive occasion, as you can see. Such colorful·

Illus. 71. Another thrilling adventure at the carnival is shown in a seventh-grader's painting, "The Roller Coaster."

**Illus. 72. "A Day at the Races" by a seventh-grader shows how strongly he was impressed. He wasn't content simply to render the race, but also the many spectators.** **This young artist is obviously interested in people and depicts them in his art in a highly individual style.**

festivals are rare in most cities and the unusual general merriment made a deep impression on the artist. It is important for young people to be exposed to unique events such as this, but remember that even a day's outing to a lake can produce a creative experience, as shown in "Swimming" (Illus. 74).

**Illus. 73. A festival left an enduring impression on a seventh-grader who visited New Orleans in Mardi Gras time.**

**Illus. 74. A tenth-grade artist spent most of his summer vacation at the beach, as shown in his painting, "Swimming."**

**Illus. 75**

# CHAPTER FIVE

# Holidays

One of the great opportunities to foster *creative art* is during a holiday season. Although almost everybody—parent and teacher—does promote increased art activities at Christmas, Halloween, Valentine's Day, etc., too often it consists of reproducing stereotyped art products. Both subjects and shapes and forms are standard. Children either copy pictures or are directed to "*Make* a turkey"; "*Make* a pumpkin"; "*Make* a Santa Claus." All of these subjects, of course, relate to a child's experience. But they rarely stand out in isolation in a child's mind—they are usually associated with certain events, situations, places, and meaningful experiences.

As an example the unusual jolly scene in Illus. 77 depicts "Christmas Morning at Grandma's." The young artist seems to be dancing around in front of the Christmas tree with her presents. This third-grader might have been asked, "What do you like best at Christmastime?" Naturally, the Christmas tree is a focal point of the holiday and she immediately recalled the joyous atmosphere of her own Christmas which she spent at her grandmother's. She did not simply draw the tree, but she reproduced the objects and activity surrounding the tree. The *feeling* that the event gave her is what she has shown in her painting. It is a painting of a Christmas tree, but not just any old tree. Rather, it is the very tree that provided her with a deep emotional experience. "*Make a Christmas tree*" would not have touched the chord in her memory that would have produced such a lively piece of artwork.

A group of elementary school children were given the opportunity to create a mural based on the theme,

**Illus. 76.**

Illus. 77. "Christmas Morning at Grandma's" shows an exciting scene in the life of a third-grader and one long to be remembered. The happiness of the occasion radiates from this painting.

**Illus. 78. Detail of Illus. 76.**

"Christmas Eve On Our Street" (Illus. 75 and Illus. 76). Their teacher encouraged each one to depict his own personal image of how the street would look to *him* and then everyone's art would be put together to form a mural that would be truly representational of Christmas. In order to get them started, a "looking walk" was arranged and the children all inspected the various

**Illus. 79. Detail of Illus. 75.**

houses on one street to get acquainted with the different kinds of decorations, as well as to review the houses themselves. The characteristics of the houses were discussed (see page 24).

The children started to work with the idea in mind that they would portray their Christmas "dream house," combining their own houses with some of the features they had seen on the walk. The teacher asked them simply "Now, think of your home. Is there anything special that your house has that other houses might not have? What did you see in the other houses that your house does not have?"

If your child had placed a laundry truck in front of his house as part of the Christmas Eve activities, would you laugh or tell him not to be silly? Illus. 79 shows a boy's rendering of his house with a laundry truck prominently parked in front. One of the first things that had entered his mind was the fact that the family would want clean clothing for Christmas Day. Perhaps this was indeed a regular experience in his life—the day before Christmas having a fresh load of laundry arrive. This is every bit a part of the festivities in this youngster's life as is trimming the tree. His personal experience thus produced a very individual piece of art. Probably no one else in the world would associate a laundry truck with the holiday spirit!

When a child does something in his art that might seem bizarre or unrelated, try to count up to 10 before mentioning it, and then do so casually, as though there were nothing "strange" about it. You will probably find out that there *is* nothing strange about it—that he has a perfectly valid explanation.

If you were to suggest that several children express their images of Santa Claus delivering his gifts, do not be surprised when they produce pictures such as in Illus. 80 and Illus. 81. Here is Santa himself in his traditional red garb arriving in a . . . *helicopter*? There is no question that a sleigh and reindeer are alien to these two fourth-graders, so it would seem perfectly natural that he arrive, not by plane either, but by helicopter, which Mrs. Santa can operate as it hovers over rooftops while Santa

Illus. 80. Santa Claus drops into the center of town from a helicopter to distribute his gifts to the awaiting children, as imagined by a fourth-grader.

Illus. 81. Mr. and Mrs. Santa make their rounds on Christmas Eve, again in a helicopter. This fourth-grader also feels that this is the most practical conveyance in a modern age.

Illus. 82. To many, the Christmas season is associated with a religious spirit as conveyed in "The First Christmas," painted by a fifth-grader. Apparently the artist is most impressed by the presence of the kings at the stable, and he has also emphasized the star which led them to the Christ Child.

completes his deliveries. This represents not only imaginative thinking, but practical considerations. These children have unwittingly expressed the growth of their reasoning powers. Since Santa must perform landing feats on mountaintops, islands, crowded city streets, and many other inaccessible places, what better means of transportation than a helicopter, and, since no one has ever really seen the sleigh and reindeer, it is perfectly possible that he does use one!

To many children Christmas has a deep religious significance. It is a time of prayer, going to church, and observing religious customs. To others, it is a time of giving and receiving presents. To still others, it is a time for perpetuating folk customs. Illus. 82 through Illus.

84 show three children's conceptions of "The birth of Christ," while Illus. 85 through Illus. 87 show different folk customs. In Illus. 85, a third-grader depicts "Selecting the Family Christmas Tree." Probably her entire family treks to the woods to choose their special tree. She has shown her tree all decorated although it is standing out in the snow. Perhaps this is the way she envisioned it would be when they came upon it in the woods. A fifth-grade student has painted "Baking the Christmas Cookies" (Illus. 86), obviously an important family ritual, while a seventh-grader portrays another age-old custom, "Christmas Carolling," in Illus. 87.

It is important to remember when suggesting topics for holidays, that, as you can probably see from the fore-

Illus. 83. A seventh-grader here portrays "The Birth of Christ" in a most individual and skilled fashion.

Illus. 84. "Madonna and Child" is a third-grader's colorful rendering of the Christmas spirit. This little artist has combined religious significance with folk customs, as the presence of the Christmas tree indicates.

**Illus. 85. "Selecting the Family Christmas Tree."**

**Illus. 86. "Baking the Christmas Cookies."**

going examples, it would be very difficult for *you* to know what specifically is of great meaning to a youngster. You must try to bring up topics that are not too general nor

too specific. They must be general enough to arouse enthusiasm, and they must not be so specific as to bypass an individual child's experience. Once you have

**Illus. 87. "Christmas Carolling."**

**Illus. 88. "Trying Out My New Roller Skates"** shows a seventh-grader and his friend trying out new Christmas presents.

**Illus. 89. The story, "The Witch Went Flying," inspired a third-grader to paint this colorful and imaginative portrayal of a most unusual witch.**

established for yourself just the right "touch," your children's art will reflect it.

Halloween is another very exciting holiday because it involves costumes, magic, witchcraft—all certain to stimulate the imaginative and creative impulses of children. You might suggest to a child that he tell you about some of his favorite Halloween or ghost stories. At the height of his excitement, a young child is bound to start dramatizing, using his hands or making faces. This is the time to say, "Joe, why don't you *make* the story for me. I'd love to see that flying witch or the green ghosts! Or any of the other things you're telling me about." Such a suggestion could result in the imaginative painting in Illus. 89. Notice how this third-grader managed to get in

all kinds of Halloween symbols—pumpkins, bats, a black cat, plus the main figure, the witch—but the painting is actually well composed. There is a light, airy feeling about it and everything "moves."

A Halloween party would provide an abundance of material for creative artwork. You could ask questions about what all the children wore, who had the best disguise, what games were played, what the decorations were like, and what they had to eat and drink. The thing that stood out in one second-grader's mind was meeting three chums on their way to the party all dressed up in their costumes. The sun is shining and the masqueraders don't look very scary. This artist has probably never experienced any of the spooky atmosphere surrounding

Illus. 90. A kindergarten artist renders his idea of Halloween and has entitled it, "I Am Happy Today." There is no question how he feels about this holiday.

Illus. 91. "The Party Fun" shows three young friends on their way to a Halloween party. This second-grade artist certainly doesn't think of Halloween as being a scary time—the sun is even shining!

Halloween. He envisions it as a cheerful, fun-filled day (Illus. 91), unlike the youngster who produced Illus. 89.

"Trick or Treat" is a Halloween activity that children love and you will be wise to bring it up as a topic. All kinds of things can happen when out ringing doorbells and scaring people with ferocious Halloween masks, to say nothing of all the goodies that go into the paper bags. There are usually more treats than tricks so that even the loot might be a subject for a drawing. Just think of the variety of cookies, candies and cakes that most children

**Illus. 92. "Trick or Treat" shows two little masqueraders carrying very large treat bags. Grade two.**

**Illus. 92A. A kindergartner shows herself making the "Trick-or-Treat" rounds done up in her mother's clothes.**

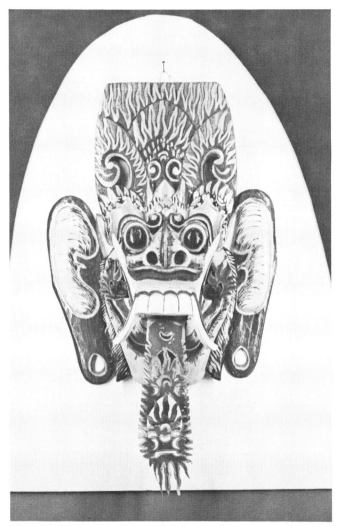

Illus. 93. Halloween immediately conjures up masks, and young artists will find it very inspiring to visit museums to see some of the fascinating masks made around the world. This dramatic ritual mask comes from the island of Bali in Indonesia and is made of wood. (From the private collection of Dr. Wilberforce W. Plummer. Photo courtesy of "Grand Rapids Press.")

Illus. 94. No less dramatic is this twelfth-grader's production, constructed from a diamond-shaped piece of corrugated cardboard composed of one vertical fold. A papier-mâché substance of facial tissue and liquid glue was used to build up the three-dimensional features such as cheekbones and nose. Red card hair adds a macabre note.

return home laden down with—such an assemblage could only happen on Halloween!

Halloween is a perfect time to inspire young people to make masks. A trip to a museum that has a collection of fascinating masks from various parts of the world (see Illus. 93) would provide great stimulus to creative mask-making. It would be interesting to ask a group of children if they know the origin of the Halloween mask. Then sketch out generally the history of Halloween and the development of masks to frighten evil spirits. Then you could ask them to name all the different kinds of masks that people use today—doctors' masks, deep-sea divers', firemen's.

**Illus. 96. A first-grade artist conveys her impression of herself in "My New Easter Dress."**

**Illus. 95. A fifth-grader constructs a paper-bag mask with cardboard ears and tempera decoration. (Photo courtesy of "Arts and Activities" magazine.)**

There are a wide variety of materials you can suggest for making masks—paper bags, papier mâché, paper plates, or cardboard.

Another dress-up holiday (but a very different kind) is Easter. A new Easter outfit inspired the first-grader in Illus. 96 to paint "My New Easter Dress," while another

61

first-grader portrayed her mother in "My Mother Dressed in New Easter Clothes" in Illus. 97. These young children have expressed the thing that impressed them the most about the Easter holiday. Perhaps they went on a shopping expedition with their mothers and were allowed to help pick out the outfits. If your child shows the same interest in portraying a member of the family in new Spring garb, you might point out that a collage using odd bits of material, paper, yarn, etc. would be a fine medium for the subject.

Easter is also the time for decorating eggs. The whole process is fascinating to children, right from blowing the egg yolk and white out through holes pierced in both ends (you can also use hardboiled eggs) to painting and dressing up the eggshell. Now is the time to get away from the old painting and dyeing procedures that everyone always does. Ask your child if he thinks it would be possible to make people and animals with the eggs. Some children might even be inspired to create drawings and paintings of the scene, "Making the Easter Eggs."

Valentine's Day immediately conjures up hearts in everyone's mind. You will probably find yourself tempted to say to your child "Clare, if you are going to make your own valentines, why not cut out one big heart and use that as a guide for cutting all the others?" Hold yourself in check! First, think of how meaningless it would be to the recipients of these "manufactured" shapes. The person receiving one, in a classroom for instance, would notice that other children had the same valentine from Clare and would find nothing special about it. Or, supposing Clare's very best friend met another child and said "Oh, Jack, look at the valentine Clare made for *me*!" Whereupon Jack says, "I got one just like it." Valentines are meant to be meaningful. They should convey a message that truly comes from the "heart."

Look at the wonderful variety of valentine cards in Illus. 98 through Illus. 101. They are all based on the heart shape, but each one is individual and shows the artist's own ideas and imagination. You can begin to stimulate such creativity by suggesting the child think of all the different sizes a heart could be; how the heart shape can be varied—tall and thin, wide and squat; or

**Illus. 97. "My Mother Dressed in New Easter Clothes" was proudly painted by a first-grader. It is doubtful if the outfit was quite this colorful, but this is the way the artist remembers it.**

Illus. 98

Illus. 99.

how the heart could be used to create other figures. Notice how a fifth-grader used the heart to make all the parts of the little figures in Illus. 100.

Other ideas you might bring about through motivation are making three-dimensional valentines by folding

or scoring (Illus. 101), or using scrap materials. The important thing is to acquaint the child with as many possibilities as you can and he will find his own special medium and way of using it. He may even develop techniques you never thought of yourself.

Illus. 100.

Illus. 101.

Illus. 102. "Run, Turkey, Run" shows a complete departure from the stereotype Thanksgiving symbols. A unique and colorful turkey and a smiling sun share the scene with the small second-grade artist. (Compare with Illus. 14 on page 13.)

Thanksgiving, which has so many overworked symbols and cut-and-dried ways of using them, is an ideal time for you to promote new creative material for children. As with the Christmas season already discussed, relate all of the Thanksgiving traditions and activities to the children's own environment and experience. For instance, the First Thanksgiving which took place in 1621 is a very difficult picture for the child to imagine. His image of it has been created by paintings and drawings he has seen in history books. Therefore, all he does when he draws the scene is imitate or copy. If he makes a turkey, he does the same thing (see Illus. 14, page 13) because he certainly has never seen the wild turkeys which ran rampant through the woods of the Pilgrims' time. Try instead to relate the *spirit* of the Pilgrims in terms of the child's everyday world.

The pilgrims were expressing their thankfulness, so you might ask a child to think of all the things he could be thankful for—his home, the clothes he has, his toys, his pets. Or you could inquire about his own celebration of Thanksgiving Day. He might produce a painting of his mother preparing the big turkey dinner, or his family gathered around the table, or even a drawing of himself and his father attending the big school football game. All of these things would express the very spirit that has been passed down through hundreds of years—not a stereotyped idea of how the Pilgrims *looked* on their day of thankfulness.

# CHAPTER SIX

# Music and Dance

Much of our everyday world is filled with music—from radios, juke boxes, television, and record players to the playing of instruments, attending concerts and dances, or the opera and ballet. Sound is a vital factor in our lives, but often we tend to take it for granted. One of the first contacts with the world for the infant is sound—before he can see clearly, he can hear acutely well. An infant is hardly able to govern his body movements, but a loud noise will cause him to jump. By the time he has reached the sitting- or standing-up stage, a child will immediately respond to music, swinging and swaying as

best he can. When he's a toddler, he marches around humming and tootling.

Therefore, music is an excellent and unusual way to promote creative art topics whether or not your child is gifted in music or dance. His everyday exposure is more than enough to stimulate him. However, it is up to you to bring out the child's musical experiences. It might never occur to him to express with crayon or paint the fact that he enjoys playing the oboe or listening to records. Or perhaps a child will express a secret desire to play an instrument or to learn to dance, as did the second-grader who painted "Kiki Loves Music" (Illus. 104).

This little girl is pretending that she is a famous trumpet player and can handle the drums as well, since she included one. Kiki's parents may never have realized her interest in music, but perhaps this artwork was produced in school under the guidance of a teacher who

Illus. 103. Third-grade students from Wyoming Parkview School, Wyoming, Michigan, listen to musical recordings. Children's records are ideal sources for motivating children in art—the music and the narration conjure up vivid mental images.

65

was inspired to use music as a class art topic. As a result, Kiki may find a trumpet under the Christmas tree! Fortunately, this little girl had been exposed in some way —whether through television or a band concert—to the trumpet and she responded to it.

You must remember always that children are limited, not by their imaginations or abilities, but by their experience. Just as their bodies need fuel, so do their minds. You never forget to give them all the vitamins and minerals and calories they need in order to grow. Try always to remember to feed their mental needs in the same way as you do their physical requirements.

If your youngster has tastes that run to wild music and dance, make use of it rather than trying to ignore it or, *worse*, disparaging it. If he really likes it, it's important to him. By the same token if you're an old Bing Crosby fan, don't get worried when your youngster starts tuning in to Beethoven. Try to encourage him to express how he feels about his cherished music or dance, whatever it may be.

In Illus. 105, a tenth-grader portrays her family—her mother at the piano—and herself and her sister in "My Musicians." Here is an instance where music obviously plays an important role, not only as an interest, but as a vital force in this girl's family life. She is expressing the fun she experiences when they all play together, certainly not a common occurence in every family where it is more usual that a single member plays an instrument or sings, if anyone at all. Her family is obviously "in tune" in every way and she likes people to know it.

**Illus. 105. "My Musicians." Grade ten.**

**Illus. 106. "Listening to My Favorite Pop Singers." Grade ten. (Photo by Marian C. Andros, Supervisor of Art, Kalamazoo Public Schools.)**

Two totally different interests in music are shown in Illus. 106 and Illus. 107. "Listening to My Favorite Pop Singers" shows the tenth-grade artist in her room enjoying the music of Peter, Paul and Mary, while Illus. 107, the work of a fifth-grader, portrays "The Bach Concert."

**Illus. 107. "The Bach Concert." Grade five.**

Illus. 108. A second-grader recalls a meaningful experience in "I Sing in the Church Choir."

Illus. 109. An unusual musical experience is shown in this fifth-grader's painting of "Christmas Carolling."

Illus. 110. "Instrumental Music" shows a ninth-grader playing in the school orchestra, undoubtedly one of his happiest activities. (See Illus. 111.)

Paintings like these can be inspired by simple questions such as: "Do you play an instrument? Do you ever go to concerts? What kind do you like best?" If the Pop fan answered simply, "Well, I just like to listen to records," would you have dismissed it as an unimportant source for art expression, but immediately have responded to the Bach fan? It is not always easy to recognize creative art experiences.

Two diverse singing groups are shown in Illus. 108 and Illus. 109. The second-grader who portrayed herself "Singing in the Choir," obviously enjoys the experience tremendously as the happy smiles tell.

A more unusual singing experience is shown in Illus. 109, "Christmas Caroling." Here a fifth-grader expresses in bold rich colors the whole spirit of his feeling about the Christmas season and the activity that he enjoyed the most—walking through the streets in the snow at night and singing under street lamps. He might have been asked by his teacher or parent what musical experience he enjoyed the most, and this immediately came to his mind. Perhaps he had never realized himself how important the experience was, particularly if he happens to be involved in musical activities all the time, such as playing an instrument or singing in the school chorus.

Another subject dear to the hearts of children and teen-agers is dancing, whether it is just swaying rhythmically to a musical beat, or classical ballet, modern dance, folk dance, or other traditional dancing. In Illus. 112, a sixth-grade girl has portrayed her image of "The Dance of the Sugar Plum Fairy" after having listened to a recording of the "Nutcracker Suite." Children's records are a marvelous source of motivating material. They are excitement of the experience in the artwork. The ballet itself is not the only thing he portrayed—rather he expressed the total experience of sitting in the theatre or auditorium. Perhaps a less dramatic event—"The School Dance"—but every bit as meaningful, is shown in Illus. 114, done by a ninth-grader. This could have been the first real dance he ever attended, but whatever the reason, this dance and the way he saw it and felt about it are expressed in his painting.

If you look at all the art in this chapter you will see how very individual it is, not only in artistic style, but in its subject matter. The main topic, of course, is music and dance, but what a wide range of expression is evident!

**Illus. 111. Another ninth-grader prefers a totally different kind of instrumental music.**

generally beautifully narrated and the special sound effects and music conjure up rich mental images, as this imaginative collage proves.

Just as with adults, some young people are spectator types and others participants. The tenth-grader who painted Illus. 113 was entranced by a ballet performance and successfully captured the color, movement and

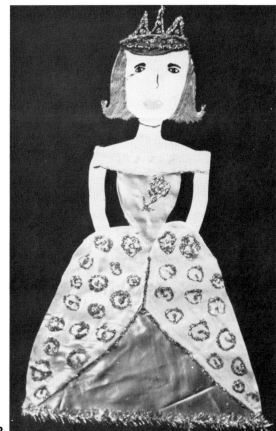

**Illus. 112.**

Illus. 113. "Attending the Ballet." A tenth-grader captures the color, movement and drama of a ballet performance.

Illus. 114. A completely different kind of dancing is portrayed in a ninth-grader's painting, "The School Dance."

## CHAPTER SEVEN

# Daily Happenings

Yesterday you had a chicken for dinner. For breakfast you had cereal, and tonight, perhaps, you will have spaghetti and meatballs. These are experiences which we all have without really thinking about them too much. Do not forget to use such daily happenings as a basis for creative art.

The sixth-grader who produced "The Supermarket" (Illus. 116) would often accompany his mother to the store, and enjoyed helping select items he liked, and carried the bundles home. However, this experience could represent a chore he wishes he did not have to do. In any event, he did it yesterday, it is fresh in his mind, and he has retained vivid images of the stock on the shelves. Notice the various weights on the sugar and flour bags. The details of this particular experience would have faded away in a short time; however, by being reminded of it soon after, it actually became a creative expression and he was able to produce an individual and very personal drawing.

When asked what she did yesterday, one third-grader produced "I And My Friend Are Making Cookies. This Is A Gingerbread Man" (Illus. 117). In spite of the fierce faces, they undoubtedly had a good time. These two friends might play together every day after school. They probably don't do the same thing each day so that such a

**Illus. 115. A third-grade boy depicts himself and his friends jumping on the trampoline in the gym—a simple everyday activity that at the moment has great meaning for him. (Photo by John Agee, Los Alamos, New Mexico.)**

Illus. 116. "The Supermarket." What could be a more ordinary experience than shopping for groceries? This sixth-grade artist obviously has strong feelings, good or bad, about accompanying his mother to the supermarket, and retains vivid impressions of the products in the store.

question will draw upon a deep well of experiences. After-school activities are always a fine source of material for art. In Illus. 118, a fifth-grade boy attended a film that thrilled him, as shown in "An Exciting Movie." Perhaps he dreamt about it all night. Notice how this child re-created not only the movie but the theatre and audience just as did the high-school student who painted Illus. 113 in Chapter 6. This is interesting because the ballet performance was certainly not an everyday event, so you might expect the total experience of being in the theatre to be portrayed; however, an after-school film once a week is a more common experience. Yet the film-goer is just as taken with the entire scene which includes the spectators as well as the film. In other words, part of the

excitement of going to the movies for this boy lies in sitting in the crowded, darkened theatre and sharing the scene before him with the rest of the audience.

One lucky eighth-grader has a Ping-pong table in his playroom, and at the moment Ping-pong games with his friends occupy a large part of his thoughts. Boys of this age are very involved in competitive sports, and yesterday might have been the crowning glory of the gang's championship games. Although he pictures a TV prominently in Illus. 119, live action is of far more importance to him. Tomorrow the Ping-pong tournaments may be forgotten and another activity or interest will replace them with just as much fervor. Children often go through periods of intense interest in one activity for

Illus. 118. "An Exciting Movie." A Saturday afternoon movie is a fairly usual pastime for youngsters, but somehow one particular occasion remains in this fifth-grade boy's mind.

Illus. 119. These boys probably can scarcely wait to get home after school every day to continue their Ping-pong tournament. A particularly exciting game is here portrayed by an eighth-grade artist in "Playing Ping-pong."

short periods of time and they never seem to tire of it until one day suddenly something else takes over. So take advantage of every day and its special meaning for a child. Illus. 121 and Illus. 122 are examples of this. The hula hoopers are portrayed by a seventh-grader and the rope jumper is a first-grader.

Another fifth-grader has a pet—a rabbit, who needs attention and occupies a part of the boy's daily activities and thoughts. Keeping his pet well fed is uppermost in his mind and this is what he is expressing in "My Pet" in Illus. 120. Although he and the bunny occupy center-stage, the background is occupied by carrots and bowls of feed and water. This child, like any other child, might neglect his pet now and then and be scolded by his parents. However, the fact that he chose to portray his pet when asked what he did yesterday indicates how meaningful the experience of running home from school to tend his rabbit is. Perhaps yesterday was the very day he forgot to do so and he is expressing his love for the little animal by holding him close in his arms.

Older children might be inspired by current events that appear in the daily newspapers. Illus. 124 through Illus.

**Illus. 120. "My Pet."** A fifth-grade boy's daily care for his little rabbit resulted in this portrait, which immediately conveys his love for the small creature.

**Illus. 121.** Here a first-grade girl proudly depicts her skill in rope jumping.

Illus. 122. At one time hula hoops were to be seen twirling round the legs, arms and heads of youngsters everywhere. This intense period of activity is captured here in a seventh-grade girl's painting of herself and her friends.

Illus. 123. The spirit and excitement of a political rally are effectively caught by a fifth-grader in his rendering entitled "IKE."

Illus. 124. After reading a news article about an escape from Communist Germany through a hand-dug tunnel, a high-schooler produced this dramatic painting of the mental image the story had conjured up in his mind. No photograph accompanied any of the stories on the following pages. (Photo by Joseph Greco.)

Illus. 125. Another exciting event is portrayed in this interpretation of the story, "Athletic Escapers Soar Free," depicting a prison break. Three shadowy figures lurk in the darkness beneath the prison wall awaiting their moment of triumph. (Photo by Joseph Greco.)

Illus. 126. A Lebanese freighter that went aground during a violent snowstorm off the coast of Norway is shown here in a vivid painting of the disaster. Although the young artist is very concerned with detail and accuracy, he has rendered the scene in a very free, expressionistic style. (Photo by Joseph Greco.)

130 were all created as the result of one high-school art instructor's idea to ask his students to select a news article that personally interested them, and which they would like to draw or paint their impressions about. He made only one stipulation—that no illustration should accompany the news item, because an actual photograph might prevent the students from conjuring up their own image of the event. Sports events, politics, violence and human-interest stories proved to be of greatest interest to most of the students, who were all in grades nine through twelve. When they came to art class they enthusiastically began to work. All of the following headlines and news stories came from *The Grand Rapids Press*, Grand Rapids, Michigan.

"The Tunnel" (Illus. 124): This article reported how a small group of people fled Communist East Germany by means of an 18-inch wide tunnel.

"Athletic Escapers Soar Free" (Illus. 125): This headline preceded a story on the escape of three prisoners from Hull Prison, England, who escaped by pole-vaulting over the wall, and inspired this dramatic painting which takes place just before the escape as the prisoners approach the wall in the dark, directly beneath a guard in his watchtower.

"Ship Aground, Vardoe, Norway" (Illus. 126): "The 1,866-ton Lebanese freighter *Michalis K* went aground off Norway during a snowstorm Wednesday. All twenty of the Greek crew were saved. The ship was considered a wreck." The young artist who painted this scene had formerly lived near the North Sea so he was able to effectively capture the character of the turbulent waters, using icy, blue-green, liquid brush strokes of paint. This boy is at an age where he is very concerned about expressing his ideas with great accuracy; for example, the two small lifeboats near the bottom of the painting contain exactly twenty survivors, and he went to some pains to research the exact character of the Lebanese flag.

"University of Michigan Students 'Elect' Romney" (Illus. 127): "Ann Arbor. In a mock election held Tuesday by University of Michigan student political groups, Republican George Romney led Democrat John B. Swainson 1,353 votes to 666. . . . The ballot boxes were set up at three campus locations and any student could vote whether or not he resided in Michigan." This painting shows a line of students waiting patiently to cast their votes. Meticulously rendered, the subject gave the artist an opportunity to use his considerable skill in figure painting as well as his imagination.

"No Matter Where Wilt Goes, Wow!" (Illus. 128): This headline refers to the famous, extraordinarily tall basketball player, Wilt Chamberlain. This comic representation points up the extreme height of the star and the futile struggle of his opponents who obviously have to "go to all lengths" to cope with him.

"Brave Lily Has Five Blossoms in Snowstorm" (Illus. 129): "Leland, Michigan. Herman Dunklow of Leland thought he was only being kind, when, after Easter, he set his Easter lily out in his backyard. During the snowstorm this week, when 3 inches of snow piled up, Dunklow discovered the lily bravely holding five large blossoms against a blustery storm off Lake Michigan." This tenth-grader was just as affected by the life-death struggle as the artist who created Illus. 130, but he was most touched by the thought of this small valiant plant weathering a killing snow. Although he shows the entire scene in beautiful detail, the lily has already started to droop—three blossoms have closed. But the vibrant life of the remaining two show hope for survival.

"Local Man Dies as Car Hits Porch" (Illus. 130): This fatal accident provided the means for a tenth-grade artist to exercise his gift for realism in his art. At this age, violence is of great concern to young people. They are becoming acutely aware of the reality of death and tragedy. Such happenings often affect them greatly.

Illus. 127. A mock election held by the University of Michigan's student body inspired a high-schooler to portray this scene at the polls. The young artist has an unusual command of several advanced techniques in art, notably perspective and figure painting, and has put them to good use in his choice of subject. (Photo by Joseph Greco.)

Illus. 128. "No Matter Where Wilt Goes, Wow!"
A sports article led to this amusing interpretation of a famous basketball star's unrivalled
advantage on the court because of his height.
(Photo by Joseph Greco.)

Illus. 130. "Local Man Dies as Car Hits Porch" reveals the emotional impact of a fatal accident on the young artist. This realistic painting conveys the immediate image the boy had when he read the headline. He managed in his stark rendering to get the idea across more effectively than if he had made a detailed painting of the scene of the accident with a car, a house, and so forth. (Photo by Joseph Greco.)

Young children might be inspired to portray current events that they see or hear about on the television news or on the radio. Or you could read to them from the daily newspaper those stories that you feel they might be able to grasp sufficiently to produce ideas for creative artwork.

Illus. 129. "Brave Lily Has Five Blossoms in Snowstorm." This human interest story inspired one artist to portray the life struggle of one small plant. (Photo by Joseph Greco.)

# CHAPTER EIGHT

# Let's Pretend

There is no doubt that make-believe is the most fascinating and prevalent activity among young people. Two-year-olds "make like a monster," 6-year-olds play cops and robbers, 12-year-olds try to emulate their heroes, teen-agers daydream and imagine themselves in a few years as parents or in a career or taking a fantastic trip around the world. Actually, make-believe continues into maturity and old age. Everyone dreams and fantasizes, and art is a perfect means of expression for young and old alike.

Very often you will find children who might be hesitant or reluctant about expressing themselves in art no matter how many creative art experiences you expose them to or bring to their attention. They might inwardly feel that the art they produce isn't "exactly like" the real thing. Perhaps at some point, a teacher or parent looked at a child's drawing and unthinkingly asked, "What's that, Mary?" Mary was embarrassed when she realized that she was expected to create something immediately recognizable to someone else. A topic relating to the world of fantasy might be just the motivational force needed to bring about an artistic creative expression from such a child.

You might suggest a topic such as "Imaginary People" or "An Imaginary Land." Illus. 131 is a first-grader's rendition of "An Imaginary Man." No one can deny the validity of this production. No one can ask, "Where is his . . . or his . . . or his . . .?" No one can say there is anything *wrong*, because this person is exactly the way he is in the little artist's mind, which is where he lives. Had this child been asked, "Draw a picture of your daddy," she might have been terribly upset that she couldn't make a faithful reproduction of her father, and given up in despair.

Illus. 131. An "Imaginary Man" is brought to life by a first-grader. The world of pretending and imagining is every bit as vivid and real as the everyday "real" world that we live in. In many cases, make-believe will bring out creative expression in young people where all else fails.

Illus. 132. Here is a wonderful example of how the use of make-believe and pretending can result in truly creative and artistic expression. With no bounds on what to draw, how to draw, what to draw with, a fifth-grader has delved into every recess of his imagination and experience. As a result, he has produced a highly personal drawing.

"I Opened My Eyes in Never, Ever Land" (Illus. 132) is a remarkably fanciful and colorfully executed piece of artwork, done by a fifth-grader. Here again, the youngster was allowed to give vent to his own world of imaginative creations. There are undoubtedly many, many creatures, objects, and people in this painting that have preoccupied the artist's fantasy world at various times and here at last he was able to put them all together, and amazingly enough, they all do go together—from denizens of the deep such as the mermaid and the octopus, to clowns, animals, and all sorts of people and things. They belong in this composition just as they belong in his own mind. This is a genuinely creative expression of this child's experience—not the experience of the world of reality, but of the world of make-believe!

"Imaginary Birds Seen from Our Spaceship" was the topic presented to a group of elementary school children whose ages ranged from 6 to 12. The results as you can see in Illus. 133 through Illus. 139 were as fantastic as the subject itself. Here is where the age-old expression "Let's Pretend" is used to its greatest advantage. The discussion began with "Let's pretend we are astronauts flying through space thousands and thousands of miles from Earth and suddenly through the windows of our

**Illus. 133. The topic, "Imaginary Birds Seen from Our Spaceship," produced this rare feathered friend conceived by a sixth-grader.**

**Illus. 134. Perhaps the thought of weightlessness in outer space gave another sixth-grade artist the idea that her imaginary bird might need a parachute.**

rocket we spy a new kind of bird—one never before seen by man. This bird is so fantastic no one on Earth will believe us if we merely describe it—we will have to draw it!"

To start off the drawing session you might ask a few

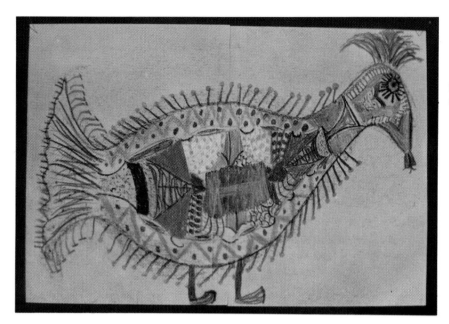

Illus. 135. Another passenger on the spaceship spotted this extraordinary bird.

Illus. 136. There seems to be no end to the assortment of birds viewed through the windows of the ship. This huge fellow dwarfs the spaceship itself! He is probably just as astounded as the spaceman.

**Illus. 137. Another imaginary bird appears to be walking on the clouds.**

**Illus. 138. This winged creature has smoke coming out of his head!**

pertinent questions concerning bird characteristics in general. "Does your bird have wings? Are they plain or fancy? Colored? Fringed? What about its beak? Is it long, short, pointed, blunt, straight, curved? Its tail? Is it plumed, short, wide? What kind of feet does your bird have? Long claws, short claws? Webbed? Imagine the kind of head such a bird could have. How about feathers? Feathers can have marvelous colors and patterns." There are many more such leading questions you can ask, but as soon as you see a child is excited enough to start drawing the vision that has come to his mind, let him go to it.

All of the imaginary birds shown here were rendered with crayon on manila paper. Before the discussion began, the children were acquainted with the many effects they could achieve with the crayon (see Chapter Fourteen). The fantasy flock shows a tremendous variety of imaginative ideas and ways of expressing them.

Since outer space is getting closer and closer to the world we live in, children and adults alike are becoming increasingly fascinated with the thought of travelling to a far planet or to the moon. Since almost everyone has watched the space flights on television, they have some idea of rockets, space suits, etc. "We Rode in the Gemini 5" is the topic that produced the drawings and paintings

**Illus. 139. One passenger on the spaceship viewed a bird swimming along contentedly. If Earth birds can swim on water, certainly space birds can swim on air.**

Illus. 140. "We Rode in Gemini 5" was the topic presented to a group of sixth-graders. The young artist who created this painting has made certain that he would not go hungry by placing a large food container in a prominent position.

Illus. 141. A detailed discussion of the interior of the spaceship reminded this artist of the many dials and instruments that would be necessary.

in Illus. 140 through Illus. 145. All of the boys and girls followed this space flight either on television or in the newspapers.

Again, the discussion began with "Let's pretend." They all talked about the kind of hat they might wear in the spaceship, what their uniform would look like. Then the discussion turned to the spaceship itself. They decided that since the capsule was small and was difficult to move about in, they should experiment with being in a confined space so they could really *feel* the

**Illus. 142. The question, "What kind of clothes would you wear on your journey?" inspired this artist to highlight his space costume.**

**Illus. 143. This artist is as concerned with the instruments as he is with the supplies. Although he has shown himself taking a lunch break, he is surrounded by a network of dials and buttons.**

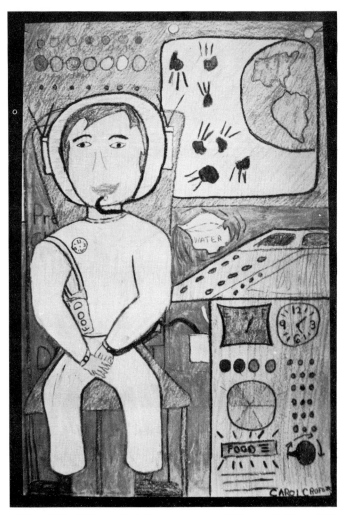

Illus. 144. A young astronaut seems most concerned with the direction the ship is taking. He is concentrating on steering, but notice he also has made a special point of including food, water and air—the vital factors for survival.

Illus. 145. This artist is as aware of the outside of the spaceship as the inside, and has included a large porthole through which can be seen the receding Earth and a shower of meteorites.

Illus. 146. Another space topic, "Astronaut on Mercury," produced an imaginative creation of an unseen planet, painted by a sixth-grader.

experience. I provided them with a large corrugated box and each of the children took turns sitting inside. Not only did they find out how it looked but how it felt. They soon began to actually relate to the experience of the astronauts. While they were in the box, they were asked about the various instruments surrounding them—dials, levers, clocks, whatever came to their mind. They became aware of the positions of their hands and legs in relation to the many parts of the capsule (see page 107).

They worked on large sheets of paper which I told them represented the limits of the capsule, reminding them how little space there was between their bodies and the walls of the ship. As a result, without exception all of the children produced artwork with a wealth of detail and imagery. The more they worked, the more they thought of missing parts—things that had come to mind when sitting inside the box, such as food and air tubes, cameras, windows. Their artwork represents an actual creative experience—they had really felt they had taken a space voyage and were able to convey it on paper. But look how individual the drawings are—no one had experienced the same thing!

Other space topics that are certain to arouse creative impulses are "Imaginary People from Other Planets"; "Imaginary Animals or Insects from Other Planets"; "Astronaut on Planet X." Illus. 146, "Astronaut on Mercury," was painted by a sixth-grader who displayed an imaginative use of color for that planet and unusual forms for the landscape. It could certainly never be mistaken for any place on Earth.

Illus. 147. "Men from Planet X," as conceived by a sixth-grader.

Illus. 148. Have you ever seen people like this? You may someday—they are "Men from Outer Space," as imagined by a fifth-grader.

Another sixth-grader in Illus. 147 has portrayed "Men from Planet X" whom he conceives as ghostlike figures, lacking features of any kind and having four arms! The colorful group in Illus. 148, created by a fifth-grader are "Men from Outer Space." Although they seem to possess recognizable features such as eyes, mouth, ears, nose, etc., they are like nothing ever seen on Earth—not even at a Halloween party!

Just as intriguing as the outer limits of the Earth is the mysterious territory beneath the land and sea. Underwater exploration, imaginary kingdoms under the sea, people, animals, fish, are rich in source material for artwork. Caves that lead to the murky depths under the rock and soil are fascinating for children to contemplate. They are almost always portrayed as being eerie and forbidding. Hidden treasures, strange people and animals have always been present in folklore dealing with the sub-surface world.

You might begin a motivational discussion that involves a story not unlike "Alice in Wonderland" where by sheer accident a child suddenly finds himself in a whole new world underground. Perhaps he could imagine he was chasing a ball and it rolled into a large hole or crack in a rock wall. Ask your child to think of all the possible ways he might suddenly find himself in a cave. He will undoubtedly get excited at the prospect, and come up with ideas and situations you would never dream of. Once he finds himself in this imaginary cave, you could ask what it is like. Is it dark? Light? Dry? Damp? Small? Large? Use the senses to guide you in your discussion—what does he *see? Feel? Hear? Smell?*

Illus. 149 and Illus. 150 are both vivid images of imaginary caves, but they are totally different. Illus. 149, done by a twelfth-grader depicts a cave that almost looks like the inside of a knothole. Perhaps he had imagined he lost something in a hole in a tree and suddenly found

himself inside and, lo and behold, he has obviously found a treasure chest! The twelfth-grader who produced Illus. 150 has found himself in a cave that could be the throat of a great giant. This eerie cavern holds an unknown terror in the form of a snake coiled ready to attack (lower right).

From the same motivational topic these two young people produced two very different pictures, not so much in the style or rendering, but in the subject—the fact that something was lying in wait inside of each of their caves, but in one case it was a happy object and in the other an evil one. Good fortune and bad fortune are the themes of these two paintings.

If you listen to children talking together, whether they are very young or teenagers, you will at one time or another hear "When I grow up, I'm going to be . . ." or

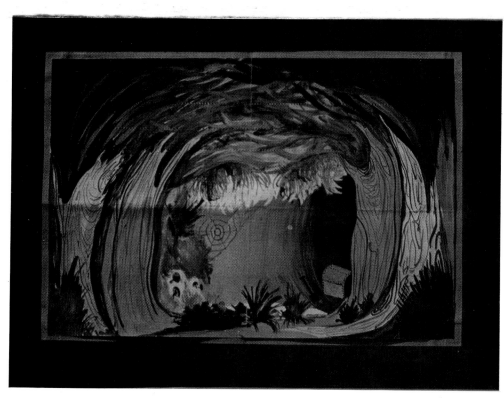

Illus. 149. The topic, "We Discovered an Imaginary Cave," inspired an eleventh-grade student to create this interesting concept of a cave. Rarely do you expect to find plants and mushrooms—you certainly hope to find a treasure chest—but this artist found both!

Illus. 150. Another rendering of "We Discovered an Imaginary Cave" produced quite a different idea. Instead of a hidden treasure, danger lurks ahead for this explorer. A treacherous snake is poised for an attack on the invader.

"I want to be . . ." Here is a wonderful opportunity for taking advantage of imaginative experiences. You can casually ask them questions about their chosen adult life—where it would take place, what they might wear, things they might use.

Illus. 151 through Illus. 157 show some of the dreams and expectations of first-, second- and third-graders. A first-grader's conception of her future role in life is depicted in Illus. 151, "I Want to Be a Beauty Operator." Perhaps a visit with her mother to the hairdresser every week has impressed her so strongly that she sees this as the most fun anyone could have after they grow up. She, as the hairdresser, seems to be happy while the client tends to look a little grim. Obviously, from her observation and experience she would prefer to be on the giving rather than the receiving end of this important event in life.

"I Am Going to Be a Scientist and Find Cures for Many Diseases" is expressed in Illus. 152 by a third-grader.

Illus. 151. "I Want to Be a Beauty Operator" stems from the topic, "What I Want to Be When I Grow Up." Grade three.

**Illus. 152. "I'm Going to Be a Scientist and Find Cures for Many Diseases." Grade three.**

Here she is seen in her laboratory conducting experiments on animals. At some point in her young life, this child has been exposed to the perils of disease and sickness for which they have found no cures, or else she might have been treated with a brand-new drug that had never been used before that cured her from a sickness. In any case, she has expressed a deep concern for saving lives, and imagines herself as a savior.

"I Want to Be a Nurse and Work in the Maternity Ward" (Illus. 153) expresses one of the most universal hopes of little girls at some time or other. However, this first-grader has pinpointed the hospital nursery as her target, probably indicating that at some time recently she visited one—perhaps to see her baby brother or sister and was so impressed with the nurses handling the tiny bundles that she can't wait to grow up and do it herself.

**Illus. 153. "I Want to Be a Nurse and Work in the Maternity Ward." Grade one.**

**Illus. 154. "I'm Going to Be a Nurse" is the promise made by a second-grader, expressing an almost universal desire of little girls. While few do actually become nurses, there is something romantic about a nurse's life and her uniform that appeals to almost all children.**

Just as so many girls want to be nurses, a great many young boys dream of becoming a doctor—and many of

**Illus. 155. Another little girl, a first-grader, also dreams of a nurse's career. Here she shows herself happily administering to the patients in their beds.**

them do, of course. A third-grader has entitled his work simply, "I Want to Be a Doctor" (Illus. 156). There are enough realistic details in this drawing to indicate that he has either been in an operating room or has taken every opportunity from television or from movies or magazines to acquaint himself with the setting of this projected self-image at the start of a difficult operation.

Illus. 157 deals with completely different expectations—"I'm Going to Be a Bareback Rider." This second-grader has nurtured the secret hope of becoming a circus performer, perhaps ever since her first visit to a circus. She may never have dared announce it before and always played safe by saying she was going to be something a little more ordinary. However, her burning enthusiasm is more than apparent in her painting—the vivid colors, the feeling of glee she has managed to express in her art. The imaginative experience in her mind has finally been brought to life.

Imaginary situations and make-believe are never-ending sources for you to provide creative art experiences for young people. Remember, in this area you yourself are limited only by your *own* "imagination!"

Illus. 156. Almost as many boys entertain the idea of becoming doctors as do girls of becoming nurses. A third-grade boy has portrayed himself here as a surgeon about to perform an operation.

Illus. 157. This young artist has often imagined herself in the exciting world of the circus and has decided "I'm Going to Be a Bareback Rider."

Stories and poems are exciting sources of inspiration for young people to express themselves in creative art as shown in this unusual diorama depicting "Jack and the Beanstalk." Grade twelve.

# CHAPTER NINE

# Stories and Poems

Stories from the world of make-believe seldom fail to stir the imaginations of young people. Young children respond to fairy tales, bedtime stories, nursery rhymes; older children through teen-age prefer adventure books, fantasy, romance, heroic tales, etc. There is no bottom to the fund of material that you can use to promote creative art experiences derived from the world of fiction.

As with the previous chapter of plain "Let's Pretend" there is no wrong way of interpreting fictional characters and events. Everyone conjures up images in their mind of stories when they read them—you gradually picture the place, the characters, etc., as the story unfolds. It would be virtually impossible not to do so. Do not, however, restrict your sources to books—there are many phonograph records that have been made of children's classics, as well as more recent additions to children's literature.

Once you have read a story or a poem to a child, immediately try to stimulate him into expressing himself artistically and creatively. Remember though, not every kind of story is going to be suitable for creative work. You must exercise your discrimination to some extent. Try to choose a story where the child can, to some degree at least, identify with the feelings and actions of the characters. Most classics are gems of human emotions—love, hate, jealousy, trust, distrust. These are all things that a child can translate into terms he understands, but you should help him.

Suppose "Hansel and Gretel" were the chosen story (Illus. 158). You might ask several children to act out the

Illus. 158. To make familiar fairy tales and stories more meaningful to young people let them take the parts of the characters and act out the stories of their choice. Creative art projects such as this diorama of "Hansel and Gretel" will almost certainly result. Grade ten.

parts of the story they liked best or that aroused their excitement the most. The principal characters are Hansel, Gretel, the Witch, and the father and mother. Remember if the drama starts to swing away from the real story, let it! It might not be recognizable as the theme at first, but in all probability the real moral of the story will come out in some way. For that matter, you may unearth a situation that exists in a child's own life that is parallel to the fairy story, even though he himself may not have realized it until the "play" began. A resulting painting or drawing would be a very personal expression of his own experience as a Hansel or a Gretel.

Another means of bringing about an individual response to a story or poem is to read up to a point just before the ending, preferably at the most exciting part and then ask your child "What do *you* think happens now?" "How would you end the story?" "Why don't you make a picture showing the end of the story?"

Dr. Seuss' "If I Ran a Zoo"[1] is a wonderful source of imaginative creations. The rhymes inevitably conjure

**Illus. 159. A sixth-grader created this imaginative diorama which represents a passage from the story, "Puss in Boots."**

[1] Seuss, *If I Ran a Zoo*, New York, 1950, Random House.

Illus. 160. "Pooh and the Piglet," as one fifth-grader envisioned them after reading A. A. Milne's classic tale, "Winnie the Pooh."

Illus. 161. An eighth-grader has created here a colorful and well-detailed diorama of a scene from "The Elves and the Shoemaker."

Illus. 162. The story of "Peter Pan" inspired a kindergartner to paint this portrait of the little boy who never wanted to grow up.

up rich mental images in children's minds. Illus. 164 through Illus. 167 are all the result of the following excerpt from this story:

"I'll go to the African island of Yerka
  And bring back a tizzle-topped Tufted Mazurka
  A kind of canary with quite a tall throat.
  His neck is so long, if he swallows an oat
  For breakfast the first day of April, they say
  It has to go down such a very long way
  That it gets to his stomach the fifteenth of May."

Can you imagine four more diverse interpretations of this bizarre bird? Illus. 165 was done by a sixth-grader who envisioned his "canary" with a peacock-like pattern, while another sixth-grader was inspired to construct his imaginary creature from papier-mâché built over a pipe-cleaner frame (Illus. 164). The second-grader's crayon drawing in Illus. 166 shows that this child was

indeed impressed by the length of the canary's throat, since the entire bird appears to be one long throat. This is a real fantasy bird created from the child's own mental images. Another section from this story is as follows:

"I'll bag a big bug who is very surprising.
  A feller who has a propeller for rising
  And zooming around making cross-country hops
  From Texas to Boston with only two stops.
  Now that sort of thing for a bug is just tops!"

This extraordinary creature produced the tissue-paper insect in Illus. 168, made by a fifth-grader. Animals and imaginary creatures lend themselves to the use of a variety of materials and media. Wire, toothpicks, pipe-cleaners, straws, clay, along with various kinds of paper and scrap materials are ideal (see Chapter Sixteen).

A book with such a wealth of imagery as the above should be read in bits and parts as motivational material.

**Illus. 164.** Dr. Seuss' "canary with quite a tall throat" is here brought to life by a sixth-grader who used papier-mâché over a pipe-cleaner frame.

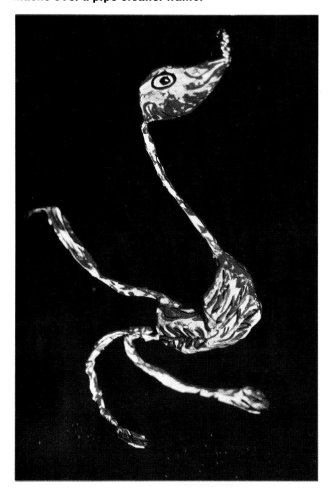

**Illus. 165.** Another sixth-grader envisioned the tall-throated canary in quite a different way.

There is so much that children might end up with a jumble in their heads. With "If I Ran a Zoo" you might concentrate on one animal at a time until you ended up with the entire zoo which could occupy a very large carton with cages made from straws and other suitable materials.

Other popular children's stories are "illustrated" in Illus. 160, Illus. 163, and Illus. 169.

A story that is ideal for providing means for children

Illus. 167. Still another interpretation of the tall-throated canary. This unusual creature has four feet and a most interesting head. This young artist was also impressed by the descriptive words, "tizzle-topped Tufted Mazurka."

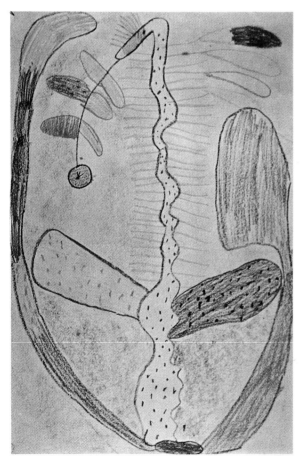

Illus. 166. A second-grade artist conveys his image of Dr. Seuss' canary as consisting almost entirely of the long throat.

Illus. 168. "If I Ran a Zoo" includes ". . . a big bug who is very surprising. A feller who has a propeller for rising . . . ," and here he is as imagined by a fifth-grader.

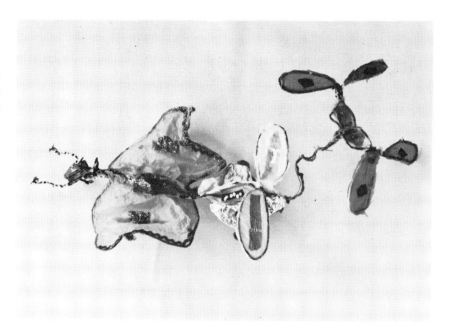

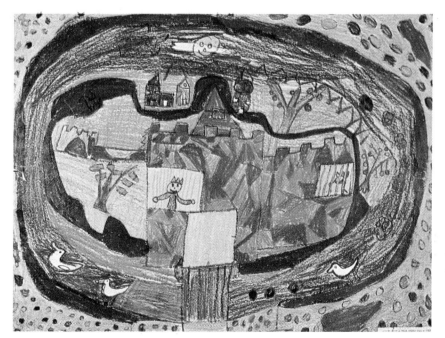

Illus. 169. The story, "Once Upon a Time There Was a Princess," provided a fourth-grader with a vivid image of the princess living in a castle on a tiny island surrounded by a moat.

from kindergartners to sixth-graders to become involved is "Giant in a Box."[2] In this story, a giant was travelling through the mountains. It was cold and snowy and night was coming on. He decided he could go no farther and looked for a place to stay. Soon he came to a village of ordinary-sized people. They came about up to his knee. The people were friendly and he asked them for shelter. They said, "We have just one vacant house in our village.

**Illus. 170. "Giant in a Box." Grade three.**

**Illus. 171. "Giant in a Box." Grade three.**

[2] Adapted from the article, "Giant in a Box," by Dorothy Powis Marcusse, *Arts and Activities,* November, 1958. pp. 38, 39, 40, 43.

But you are so large, we will have to remove a whole wall to get you in." He curled himself up inside, being careful to get all of him in out of the cold. He had to crouch in such a way that his knees touched his chin. The villagers helped by pushing the giant until every part of him was inside. It was rather crowded but the giant had a place to spend the night safe from the raging storm.

As in Chapter Eight, page 91, I provided a large corrugated cardboard box for my students to sit in (Illus. 172). Everyone tried it and they saw how the giant

Illus. 172. A fourth-grader demonstrates for his classmates the body position of an enormous giant enclosed in a small house while the author looks on. (Photo by Don Chrysler, Principal, Central Elementary School, Grandville, Michigan.)

Illus. 173. A third-grader renders his image of the giant. His long curly-toed boots may have had to be curled just to fit into the house.

Illus. 174. A fifth-grader shows his giant doubled up inside the house and he is obviously happy he is finally out of the storm. This giant was imagined as a kind of ragged vagabond and is dressed almost like a person who has been shipwrecked and living on a desert island. He even has a beard and pirate earrings.

Illus. 175. Another fifth-grader used a horse-shoe shape as the base for the position of the giant, and it worked well, as you can see. This giant is also pictured as being a poor fellow—he has ragged pants and sleeves and patches on his clothing.

**Illus. 176.** An exciting story or poem is bound to stimulate youngsters to express themselves creatively in art. Try to select material rich in imagery. There is so much available that you should have no trouble unearthing stories that will strike responses in every child.

might look as well as how he felt. The giants that were produced were tremendously varied as the illustrations show. Some giants were crouched, some weren't; some were standing, some were sitting; some faced sideways and some face front. Obviously, none of the children had felt the same way in the box. The youngest children (Illus. 170 and Illus. 171) showed their giant standing up; however, he *was* squashed within the confines of the paper.

Older children, fifth-graders, (Illus. 174 and Illus. 175) did show the figure doubled up as well as filling the paper. However, it doesn't matter exactly how they interpreted the motivational preparation because they all produced individual artwork which represented their very own imaginative processes. There was no mention of the giant having three heads (Illus. 171) but that does not mean that he didn't. This was the image that immediately came to this child's mind, for whatever reason and it stuck.

As you can see, the more you are able to stir up the imaginations of children by graphic presentations of stories or poems, the richer and more exciting will be their creativity. Use such means for all kinds of stories and tales, from biblical accounts of "Noah and the Ark" and "Jonah in the Whale" to "The Three Little Pigs" and "Cinderella" to modern-day "Superman" or "The Lone Ranger." Your job is to unearth the things that will unleash a child's creative expression.

# CHAPTER TEN

# Through a Looking Glass

Nature is without doubt one of the most inspiring sources for creative art. Let's think of all the *little* things in nature—the beauty there is in just one rose or one ladybug. Children love magnifying glasses or microscopes —a vast new world is opened to them. They see things they never knew existed—the delicate etching of a fly's wings, the multiplicity of detail that the naked eyes never pick up. Even a drop of water is fascinating under a magnifying glass or microscope!

A magnifying glass is the most practical for younger children. First, take your child for a "looking walk"— you need go no further than the garden, or if you are a real city dweller, a flower box or a single potted

**Illus. 177.**

**Illus. 178. A magnifying glass opens up a whole new world—plants and insects suddenly come alive and are "seen" by children for the first time. Spiders, bees, ants take on new colors and shapes; plants assume patterns** and hues never imagined! Such enlightening experiences are certain to provide source material for genuinely creative art expression. (Photo by Frank Mulvey. Courtesy "School Arts" magazine.)

**Illus. 179. "Catching Butterflies with Nets"** shows a fifth-grader and her friend. Look at the size of the butterflies! After viewing the small creatures through a magnifying glass, the artist now wishes to portray them the way they really look.

plant will do. If you do go into the garden or woods, find a peaceful spot to just sit quietly and observe the plant and insect life around you. You may be astonished yourself at the busy world that exists in just a few square feet of soil.

Talk about the different plants, the grass, whatever insects you might spy until the child starts to get really interested and excited. If he suddenly points to a flower and says "Oh, look!" this is the time to bring out the magnifying glass. He will probably be so fascinated by the unexpected close-up he will start going from plant to plant, taking a close look at such things as tree bark, moss, grass, or whatever else comes to his attention.

During the course of this investigation insects are bound to appear under the magnification—large ones such as caterpillars, bees, beetles or tiny ones such as aphids and ants. Discuss the various colors, textures, and shapes. Notice how the colors of tiny creatures appear different when magnified. What looks black may really be blue, what looks like a solid color might be speckled or striped. Shapes are different, too. A circular shape might actually be round, a flat form might in reality be three-dimensional. Encourage children to touch the plants and insects that he finds—what appears smooth might be furry, or what seems soft could be hard.

If your child is a collector, as most children are, you might bring along a collection box. Avoid capturing live insects if possible. All children love to catch butterflies and beetles, but try to find some that are already dead for the collection. If you take a butterfly net, examine the little creatures while they are in the net and release them as soon as possible. You will find many dried specimens are already available if you look hard enough. In any event, the wonder of the enlarged blossoms and bugs will make a deep impression on your child, and since you are not seeking to teach him to *copy* nature, the images that he carries home with him are the important thing. You will have provided him with a treasure trove of experience for creative art.

You might start a "Beauty Box," a collection of interesting rocks, unique flowers, odd-colored-and-shaped leaves, berries, shells, starfish, dried specimens of

**Illus. 180. "Moss Scales through the Magnifying Glass." New colors, shapes, and textures were discovered in moss by a fifth-grader when he examined it under the magnifier. He was inspired to create this colorful, interesting design in crayon.**

all kinds. Use a large carton cut down so that the sides are approximately 2 inches high and line it with a soft felt or cotton material which has a nap so that the articles will not slide around. When a rainy day comes along, this will serve as an "indoor looking walk"! Remember though, don't sit a youngster in front of the box and have him copy. Tell him to examine to his heart's content and then bring his impressions to his artwork. Encourage him to use a variety of media. The qualities that are brought out through a magnifying glass or a microscope—texture, dimension, etc.—are especially suitable for collage or other techniques (see Chapters Thirteen through Sixteen).

Illus. 181 and 182 show two youngsters' impressions of looking through the magnifying glass. Illus. 181, "Cattails, Flowers and Butterflies," was done by a sixth-grader and is particularly interesting because the root system of the plants is shown in very fine detail. Obviously this child, through the magnifying glass, had suddenly observed the lovely structure of many roots, and when creating what appears to be at first glance a surface representation of the plants, he brought his strong impressions of the "hidden" portions to his drawing. The plants no longer seemed complete to him without their roots. Most of the plants shown are water lovers—lily pads, cattails, ferns.

Illus. 182, on the other hand, is a pure representation of the other end of the plant system—the blossoms. There are no stems, just a mass of flowers. This third-grader has conveyed her special vision through the magnifying glass in the title, "Flowers, Flowers Everywhere." She was delighted with the tremendous diversity of petals and colors, and this experience is brought out in her chalk drawing. Certainly such a colorful massing of flowers would occur rarely in nature, but the child was able to create it in art.

A variety of insects is shown in Illus. 183 through Illus. 187. At first glance, Illus. 183 looks like a big colorful owl, and that's what "The Beetle Bug" looks like through the magnifying glass! Can you imagine the

Illus. 181. "Cattails, Flowers and Butterflies." It is obvious from the delicate detail of the various plants, that this sixth-grader was fascinated with what he viewed through his magnifying glass.

surprise this sixth-grader had when he *really* saw the beetle for the first time?

A spider web (Illus. 185) fascinated a tenth-grader who was caught by the delicate beauty of the web and the spiders. He became aware of the hues of these small creatures and was so struck by the seemingly small variations that he intensified the colors to pure blues, reds, greens, and yellows. All the tiny details—hair, striations etc., are heightened in this "fanciful" representation of what he saw under the magnifying glass. Yet, it is in fact, what he *did* see. Looking casually at a spider web, one imagines it is quite colorless or certainly doesn't think in terms of color. But when this boy became aware of the existence of color he was inspired to render this creative painting.

Illus. 182. This artist was impressed most by the variety of colors and shapes. She has expressed her impressions in a lovely floral arrangement.

**Illus. 183. Did you know this is the way a beetle looks under the magnifying glass? When this sixth-grade artist actually saw one his awareness was heightened, and he portrayed the beetle as brilliantly colored and enormous in proportion to the flowers surrounding him. Although the colors are probably not true to life, the artist chose to emphasize them because he previously had thought that beetles were black.**

An insect collection is depicted in crayon-resist (see page 148) in Illus. 186. This fourth-grader has successfully combined a variety of different elements into a well-balanced design, rather than making a representational "picture." Notice how naturally the parts are linked one to the other by overlapping, barely touching, or through the use of color. The legs of the insects are all stylized and none of the parts are as they appear in nature. This is a genuinely individual piece of art—imaginative, and showing the artist's very personal outlook. His choice of the crayon-resist technique which is ideally suited to the subject is another reflection of his imaginative processes.

**Illus. 184. "Beetles and Ladybugs," rendered in crayon by a fifth-grader, reveals his magnified view of the insect world.**

Illus. 185. "The Spider Web" shows a tenth-grader's close-up of an unusual variety of spiders. One spider looks more like a fly who might have become tangled in the web by accident!

Illus. 186. An insect collection is here created using the crayon-resist technique (see page 148), forming an interesting design.

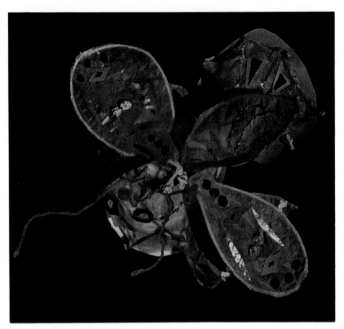

**Illus. 187. A nonscientific insect was created by a fifth-grader who used tissue paper and pipe cleaners to convey the delicate structure of a magnified bug. Notice how the Christmas glitter and other decorative accents impart the feeling of iridescence, a quality of most real insects.**

There is such a multitude of objects that offer new vistas when viewed through a magnifying glass. Sea life and bird life are combined in "Shells and Feathers Through the Magnifying Glass" in Illus. 189, rendered by a fifth-grader. Another form of sea life as seen through the magnifying glass is shown in "Starfish" in Illus. 188, done by a fourth-grader. It is interesting in both of these drawings that as in Illus. 185, all nuances of color or hues are portrayed in full color. Again, this is certainly not the way these objects appear to our eyes ordinarily, but they represent the awakening of these children to the world of minutiae.

The junior-high school boy in Illus. 191 has unearthed still another world beyond that of the simple magnifying

glass—that of the microscope. His findings are shown in Illus. 192. Science study which brings new dimensions into a young person's life is an excellent means for stirring up creative expression. This boy could easily be at a loss for words to convey what he felt when he saw the color, texture and movement of the specimen beneath the lens, but he was able to produce an abstract crayon-resist drawing that expressed this experience.

Still another "looking glass" that you might use to promote unusual art experiences is the telescope, which would reveal small sections of the heavens—gaseous nebulae, galaxies, star fields, or would even bring into a child's view a close-up of a bird singing in a tree (Illus. 190). Draw upon all of the fields of nature that you can think of to provide your child with new and exciting material. Every door you open will provide rewarding experiences for both you and your child.

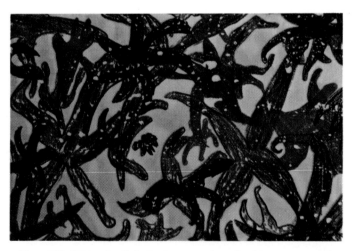

**Illus. 188. This starfish design was inspired by a youngster who kept a collection of such items in his "Beauty Box." The drawing actually gives an impression of being a view underwater, the natural habitat of live starfish.**

Illus. 189. No! It is not a carnival scene. This is how "Shells and Feathers through a Magnifying Glass" looked to a fifth-grader.

Illus. 190. A rare bird is caught unawares by a kindergartner through the powerful lens of a telescope.

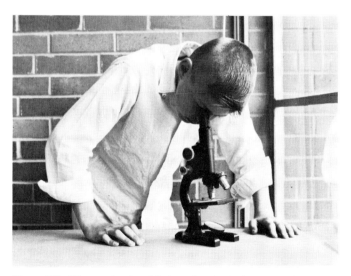

Illus. 191. Tim, a junior-high-school student, studies the unusual lines, shapes, colors and textures of a stained specimen through his microscope. What did he find? See Illus. 192.

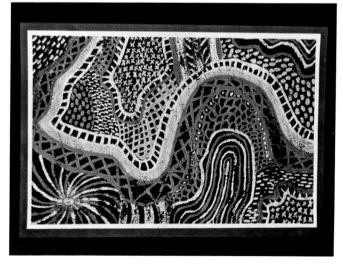

Illus. 192. Tim came away from the microscope with a vivid impression of the specimen and rendered it in a technique he felt best suited his ideas—crayon resist.

# CHAPTER ELEVEN

# Beyond the Lollipop Tree

Illus. 193. Do you know the lollipop tree? You should. Almost every young child develops this rigid symbolic form.

Have you ever noticed just how often trees are included in children's paintings and drawings? It is not really surprising because the tree has long been a popular subject or element in all art. It is represented almost as much as is the self-image, which we will discuss later. For this reason, it is necessary and important to consider it in any discussion of creative art.

If you do not know what the lollipop tree is, you will undoubtedly recognize it in Illus. 193. This second-grader has produced an almost perfect example of the geometric type of tree that appears in young children's first efforts to make representational objects. Here is the long rectangular brown trunk topped by the green circle. Now look at Illus. 194 through Illus. 202, all done by second-graders! *What has happened?* Very simply, these second-graders have become *creative* artists. Their art shows an increased awareness of an object—the tree— that was as familiar to them as anything in their lives.

Between the ages of 4 and 7, children begin their first attempts to represent trees, and they develop a "schema," or concept, which is usually geometric as shown in Illus. 193. Sometimes there are variations such as a thick rectangular trunk with a few lines extending from the top in a semi-circular arrangement, but generally the "lollipop" tree appears. From 7 to 9 years of age this schema becomes more and more pronounced. The child arrives at a rigid concept and repeats it over and over again. What he is actually doing is portraying only what his *active* knowledge allows him to express.

Your task essentially is to increase his active knowledge, to bring out a deeper awareness of the tree and pave the way for the child's very own personal expression of the subject. In order to do this, you must provide the proper stimulation in the form of experiences that will allow the child to bring his *emotional* responses to the tree to his artwork. You will find, as with everything else,

Illus. 194. Can you believe that this tree was drawn by a second-grader, perhaps the same one who drew Illus. 193? Where is the old lollipop that is so typical of this age?

Illus. 195. This second-grade artist's new-found aware-ness led to a completely different concept of trees. His tree is full of texture and color and he has included a squirrel, a rabbit, and a dog in the picture.

the more experiences you are able to provide, the more his concept of the tree will be enriched.

Now, how do you approach a creative art experience involving a tree? Perhaps you yourself have a rigid image of trees and would produce something very similar to the child's or else you would feel it necessary to *copy* a complex tree in order to avoid the stereotyped symbol.

**Illus. 196. This young artist was most impressed with the discovery of knotholes and pine cones which dominate his drawing.**

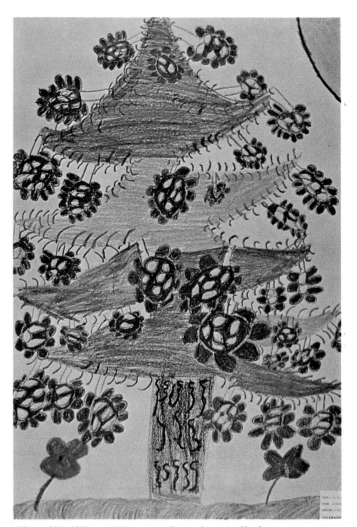

**Illus. 197. When this second-grader studied an evergreen tree on his looking walk, he was unconsciously impressed with the pine cones, and he exaggerated their proportions in his drawing.**

Certainly the most effective means of providing an enriching experience is to take a "looking walk." Even if you live in a city, there are parks or isolated trees that have been planted by the city along the streets. A looking walk will allow a child to use all of his senses. He will be able to see, feel, hear and smell different kinds of trees, and may suddenly become aware of trees as living creatures. Perhaps they always looked as dead as furniture

Illus. 198. Here's a lively tree! Filled with color and movement, the tree of this second-grader is teeming with all kinds of animal and bird life.

Illus. 199. Nothing could be further from the traditional lollipop tree than this colorful, unique tree produced by a second-grader who obviously drank in all that she saw on the looking walk and has expressed it in her art.

Illus. 200. "The Tree Seems to Stretch All Over" is the title this second-grade artist gave his painting. He suddenly became aware of the magnitude and growing power of trees.

Illus. 201. Discussion of trees and their environment led to this conception of a tree by a second-grader who shows in his drawing, "Raking Leaves," still another aspect of trees. He has shown a relationship of people and trees. He could have shown a tree house, someone climbing a tree or a swing hanging from one of its branches.

122

to a child because his concept of living was restricted to human or animal life. This by itself would be a wonderfully enriching experience.

Because trees do not exist in isolation, before you concentrate your discussion on the trees themselves, it might be well to start with observing the environment, or the "residence," of the trees. In this way you will move from the general to the specific. There is little point in studying a twig of one branch on one tree before you look at the whole picture. That would be rather like opening a book, reading one page, and then writing a book report on the entire book. The page would certainly not convey an over-all deep image of the story. You would have few impressions and mental images. In effect, your report would be a kind of written lollipop tree—a limited fixed idea. The old expression "he can't see the forest for the trees" is precisely the point here.

Start your discussion with such questions as "Where do you find trees? What kinds of things do you usually find near trees? Trees in the city have different settings from trees in the country. Can you think of what differences there are? Start with country trees. Does anyone use these trees? Do animals use trees? Have you ever seen cows and horses huddled under trees because it's shady or because it's raining? How about city trees? Do you use them? Does anyone else use them? How?" By this time you will have started getting many answers! The child will suddenly remember all kinds of things about trees that he has seen. Trees in meadows. Trees in forests. Trees in rainstorms. Picnics under trees. Squirrels running up and down. Birds flying in and out. Birds' nests. Horses scratching themselves on the rough bark. A cat that got caught on a high limb. Swings. Beehives. Old trees. Young trees. Keep the discussion going and things will keep pouring out.

Move the topic from the park and fields to backyards and trees close to home. "What trees do you have living near your house? Do you climb them? Do you have a treehouse? What kinds of trees are they? Maples or evergreens? Do you have a birdhouse? Have you ever raked leaves? Which trees look different in summer than in winter? Have you ever seen such creatures as caterpillars, praying mantises or spiders on your trees?"

Once the child has become aware of the multitude of things surrounding trees—animals, plants, people, buildings, insects, birds, turn his attention to individual trees.

**Illus. 202. A tree's environment might include a fence and a house, as well as some friends, such as birds and squirrels.**

Illus. 203. "Can a tree do anything? Does it move? Can you imagine how it feels to be a tree?"

Illus. 204. "Let's pretend we're trees and the wind is blowing against us. Our legs are close together like a thick trunk. Our arms can be the branches and our fingers the twigs."

Illus. 205. On your looking walk, notice all the different kinds of trees, and talk aloud about them. Touch them, smell them, run around them, climb them. Observe their setting and how the sun makes some trees light, others dark.

On your walk, pick out different kinds of trees to discuss and compare. "This tree seems especially large. See how long it takes to run around it! Some of those branches are as big as trees themselves. Can you see how the branches get smaller near the top? Why is that? Feel the bark. Is it rough or smooth? Can you see what kind of leaves it has? There's a knothole. Do you suppose someone lives in there? A squirrel? A bird? What a tremendous shadow this tree casts. Some of the leaves look darker than others. Is it because they are on the shady side right now? When the sun moves around, will they look light? Does this tree have a particular aroma? Now, let's find a small tree."

By this time, children will start running from tree to tree, making all kinds of discoveries. One tree is tall and thin, another wide and spreading, another has nuts or berries. One has broken branches; another has new buds. The great variations in trees will suddenly become a reality to a child at this stage. Once he becomes aware of the individuality of each tree, turn your discussion to the nature of the life of trees. Ask: "Can a tree do anything? Does it move? Can you imagine how it feels to be a tree? Let's pretend we're trees and the wind is blowing against us. Our legs are close together like a thick trunk. Our arms can be the branches and our fingers the twigs.

"Here comes a breeze from the left! What do you feel? Another one is coming from the right! Now from the rear. What is happening to your branches? Your twigs? Your trunk? Do you feel like groaning the way trees do in a heavy wind? Or do you feel creaky?

"It's started to rain. Now, how do you feel? Droopy or happy? Some trees love the rain. They drink it up as fast as they can. What colors are you wearing today? Your new green spring outfit? Or your fall cloak of many colors? Or your white winter blanket? Are you wearing perfume? Is it sweet or is it musky? Do you like being a tree?" You can expect a certain amount of giggling and self-consciousness at first, but you will be more than rewarded when the child really starts to feel the role of the tree.

As I have said earlier, make the looking walk for young children a pre-art session experience, and for older youngsters, conduct an out-of-doors drawing period. During the "gang age," from 9 to 11, children become more articulate and more accurate in their expression. You will find during this period a child will make a great effort to portray the tree in a more realistic way. The early stylized geometric symbol gives way to imitation, and here again you must do all you can to avoid so-called photographic imitations. You should continue to foster his creativity in terms of his personal experience.

You will find two distinct approaches during this age period and during later adolescence. Some children portray their subject as a *visual* concept only, others as a *subjective* experience. The visually minded child is very concerned with color, lights and darks, and perspective as they relate to his subject. A perfect example of this is shown in the crayon drawing, "Tree Near Playground"

(Illus. 208), done by a sixth-grader. This boy has meticulously shown the scene exactly as it appeared. He views the subject as a spectator and his emotions simply do not enter into the picture. This is an "observed" representation. He has fulfilled all the requirements he set out to meet to the best of his technical abilities, and has done quite well. However, this environmental tree scene could easily have been copied from a photograph.

Now look at Illus. 209, "Winter Evening Sky," painted by a fifth-grader. Without setting out to do so, this child also fulfilled the artistic demands of perspective, lights, darks, etc., but this artwork is the product of an emotional response to the subject. He has expressed a mood that reaches out and makes you not only a spectator but a participant. You can *feel, hear* and *see* the wind howling through the trees and the driving snow. Notice how he has splattered white paint on the paper and run white streaks in different directions, conveying the confusion

**Illus. 206. The twelfth-grader who painted this woods scene is interested in color, perspective and lights and darks.**

Illus. 207. "In the Park in Autumn." Older children will benefit from painting on the spot. They are better able to cope with eliminating unnecessary detail and finding a focus of interest around which to work.

Illus. 208. "Tree Near Playground," a crayon drawing by a sixth-grader, is an example of an "observed representation." The artist has carefully rendered his subject exactly as he sees it.

Illus. 209. "Winter Evening Sky," painted by a fifth-grader, is an expressionistic portrayal of the subject. The artist was not concerned with painting the scene exactly the way it looked; rather, his emotions took over and he has captured the mood of the snowstorm.

of the storm. He has beautifully captured a moment of turbulence and shown his own personal feelings and outlook at the same time. You know the moment you look at this painting that the young artist was very involved in his work emotionally.

Both approaches are, of course, artistically valid, but what we are trying to do in this book is to promote creativity in young people based on their emotional experiences. Sometimes the results are artistically beautiful as in the case of Illus. 209 and sometimes they are not. Sometimes the young artist who copies produces a piece of art more conventionally acceptable, but as I said in the beginning of the book, our concern should not be with technical proficiency but with personal expression and release of a child's mental images. Art has a place in everyone's life and you must dispel from children's minds that there is a "good and bad" or a "right and wrong" way of drawing, painting, sculpting, or creating in any media.

Now, look how far *you* have progressed beyond the lollipop tree!

# CHAPTER TWELVE

# Life Drawing

As we saw in Chapter One, a very young child's first scribbles with a pencil or crayon are most often his image of "Mommy." Therefore, the human figure is really the subject of almost all first efforts to draw. As a child approaches 4 or 5 years of age, the figure is often likely to be a self-image. All children during the early years are egotistical in the sense that the world revolves around them and their needs.

After the toddler stage of scribbles and blobs, geometric forms begin to appear—mainly circles and squares. The human form is generally concentrated around the head in children's drawing so that you find the figure consisting of a large round head and two legs as in 4-year-old Aimee's pencil rendering of "I Have Big Eyes" (Illus. 210). Aimee has however added two very small arms. Notice how she has made an attempt to depict feet by making large indentations which represent toes.

Your approach to creative art experiences in developing a deeper concept of the human figure is of great importance. First of all, the figure is one of the most difficult subjects to render. Artists spend lifetimes studying and developing their techniques in this field, and you must never make a child feel incompetent if he produces a "wrong" figure—even one without hands or feet, for instance. Technical accuracy will take many, many years to develop; however, you do want to do all you can to enrich a child's concepts concerning the body—its parts, how they work, etc., in order to avoid the repetition of a rigid figure pattern.

The more aware a child becomes of the complexities of the figure, the greater will be his ability to produce imaginative, even exaggerated, renderings of it, which however will probably be closer to "reality" than his fixed schema. He will learn to express the *qualities* of

**Illus. 210. "I Have Big Eyes" says 4-year-old Aimee in her drawing. Children of this age are most likely to represent the human form in geometric shapes, such as circles and squares. Aimee has done very well for her age by adding arms and toes.**

the human body—dimension, movement, flexibility, expressiveness.

If your very young child continually makes a figure with certain parts missing, such as the arms, the legs, or the trunk, you might draw attention to the missing member by saying, "Let's stand in front of the mirror. Wave your

Illus. 211. Linda, who is in kindergarten, has made great strides by having not only a head but a body, arms, legs, hands and feet. She has entitled her work "I Am Painting," and it is obvious that she enjoys this activity, judging from the big smile and the presence of a radiant sun.

arms! Kick your legs! Wiggle your feet! Wiggle your hands! Twist your shoulders! Twist your hips!" Body activity helps children become aware of their individual parts in action, and this indirect method of stimulating them to make new discoveries is far more exciting for them. Suppose you were to say in a rather scolding fashion, "For heaven's sake, Joe, you know you have elbows. Where are they in your drawing?" You would most certainly elicit a negative reaction from Joe. He would most likely be embarrassed and would feel inhibited rather than excited about the subject of elbows.

The vital thing to remember is that although you want to provide experiences for the child that will give him a deep awareness of the body, you must not expect nor demand a faithful representation.

Since the self-image is so important to young children, art topics will be most meaningful when they involve the child. An example of this is shown in Illus. 211, "I am Painting," drawn by Linda, a kindergartner. Linda has included her major body parts and is also involved in an activity. You will find that most drawings during these years are entitled, "I . . . " Therefore, when suggesting topics, always try to stimulate the child by conducting a pre-drawing experience where the child actually performs the act—"I Am Kicking A Ball," "I Am Eating." These

little pantomimes are not only fun for the child, but provide an invaluable insight for him into the action that really takes place.

Such experiences might lead him to exaggerate the important parts of his body during certain activities. Eating might result in a very large mouth and a big arm bringing the food to it or an emotional response might be exaggerated such as in Linda's drawing. She obviously enjoys painting and has produced an enormous smiling face.

Encourage the child to see the figure in relationship to his environment. For instance, if he is jumping rope, ask him *where* he is doing it—on the sidewalk, in the gym. Ask him *what* other things are around him—objects, people, animals. In this way a child will develop an enriched concept of the human form, that is, he will not think of it in terms of a rigid isolated symbol but as a flexible, dynamic force.

By the age of 9, or on a fourth-grade level, children are very concerned with a realistic portrayal of the human figure. The early geometric lines which characterize the figures of younger children no longer please the young artist. He sees the figure as ever-moving, ever-changing. Now he wants to adjust his representation to correspond to nature. At this stage you can introduce a live model.

Illus. 212. After a long search the child arrives at a figure concept which is complete in detail. At this stage of development you must work at motivating a child to express his concept in a more flexible way. Grade two.

Illus. 213. By the time the child reaches 9 or 10, he begins to see the human figure as a moving object, and becomes very interested in depicting the subject in action. This fifth-grader has shown all of his figures walking rigidly. At this point, a live model will heighten this child's awareness of joints, such as knees, elbows, and ankles, that are involved in body movement.

**Illus. 214. Pieces of torn construction paper in the general shape of parts of the body are excellent to use in beginning a study of a live model. As the model changes position, the child can move the various parts about to represent the poses. Grade four.**

When you pose your model, preferably another child who will also gain by the experience, point out all the moving parts the human body has. Ask your model to assume a running pose, a jumping pose, sitting, bending over, kneeling.

One of the most effective means of teaching a child to observe a model is by the use of torn construction paper as shown in Illus. 214. One piece can represent the head, another the torso. Three separate pieces can make up the parts of the leg or arm. As the model changes position, the child can rearrange the torn paper shapes to suggest the various action poses. After a number of poses have been completed, he can paste all the pieces in place on a sheet of contrasting colored construction paper to simulate the pose that interested him the most. This activity gives the child a chance to see how the body is capable of assuming an almost infinite variety of positions.

Immediately following the tearing and pasting activities is the right time to start to discuss painting or drawing figures in action. Now bring up the environment of the active figure by asking *where* the figure is running, jumping, sitting, or whatever.

Illus. 215 is the work of a fourth-grader who besides showing himself in action in "I Am Playing Basketball" has shown where he is playing as well. As we can see, he has a basket over the garage doors, and the feeling that he has for this special activity includes the setting—his house, the tree, the fence—even a squirrel spectator. He has conveyed an emotional warmth about the surroundings where he enjoys himself—an image that will probably live with him when he grows up. He will remember not just the enjoyment of the game but the place where he played it. If you think about it, almost everybody has such images of their childhood. Environmental settings may become distorted with the passage of time, but the *atmosphere* remains.

There are several approaches to figure drawing that you can use very effectively for youngsters from grades five through twelve.

*Action Drawing* (Illus. 216 and Illus. 217): The action drawing is very quickly executed. Using the model as shown, ask the artists to render a quick line impression of the figure in action, leaving out all small fussy details. This is an excellent means of causing a youngster to see the figure in its entirety. You can use more than one model for action drawing—two models in boxing or dancing poses, three or more "sitting in a car" or at a dining table. The group offers an interesting variety of poses, because even though they might all be doing the same thing, they will all do it differently.

*Gesture Drawing* (Illus. 218—Illus. 220): This is also executed briefly with poses lasting no longer than five minutes. The gesture drawing places emphasis on the mass or solidity of the figure. The term "gesture" refers, not to the model, but to the kind of hand movements the artists use to draw the action figure. Continuous loops or ovals as shown in Illus. 220, or zigzag lines as shown in Illus. 219, or any other kind of scribble effects can be used to convey the figure's bulk. You will find that most young people really enjoy using the free motions associated with this approach. A gesture drawing can start at any point. Some children begin with the head and work down; others start with the biggest part—the torso—and then add the head and limbs. There is no rule about how to make a gesture drawing.

*Silhouette Drawing* (Illus. 221 and Illus. 222): When creating a silhouette drawing, the artist portrays the active figure as a solid black form. Using black tempera, charcoal, India ink or dark crayon, the model is represented as a solid mass. The center of attention is placed upon the outside edges of the figure. There is no distraction from details such as lines and patterns. If tempera is used, the artist can start with a small puddle of paint in the middle of the paper which can then be "pulled" with the brush to create the bulk of the figure. The most effective way to create silhouette drawings is to make them large. Approximately 10 to 15 minutes should be allowed for each drawing.

*Memory Drawing* (Illus. 223, page 137): In making

**Illus. 215. Follow up the torn-paper activities with artwork representing the figure in action. Here a fourth-grader has depicted himself playing basketball in his back yard. Although his arms are still rigid, he has discovered that his knees bend.**

Illus. 216. Action Drawing. At the fifth-grade level, children like to view the model as they draw. Action poses of 4 to 10 minutes allow sufficient time for studying the position and completing a drawing.

Illus. 217. Have the model stand on a table top and assume an action pose. The artists themselves can assume the same pose as the model in order to "feel" it before commencing to draw.

Illus. 220.

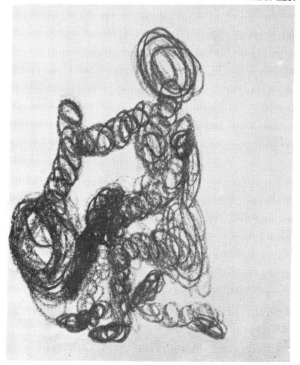

Illus. 218. Gesture Drawing. This technique refers not to the model but to the hand movements that the artist makes—scribbles, lines, etc., as shown in Illus. 219 and Illus. 220.

a memory drawing, have a model pose in an action position. Ask the artist to observe the figure very carefully. Emphasize the importance of the total figure, not the details. Tell the child to "draw" the figure with his

**Illus. 221. Silhouette Drawing. Here the focus of interest is the outline of the figure. The mass of the body is filled in with solid black as shown in Illus. 222. Allow 10 to 15 minutes for each pose.**

eyes. Then the model leaves the stand and the artist proceeds to draw from memory. Encourage him to concentrate on his general impression and image. The result should be a very personal expression of the artist's feeling toward both the figure and the action.

*Contour Drawing:* This is another term for an outline drawing. Have your young artist focus his attention completely on the model at the same time as he creates a line drawing expressing the contour of the figure. *He must not look at the drawing at any time.* Allow at least 15 minutes for completing each drawing. You might help by suggesting a starting point, for instance, the head. Then ask him to make a "round trip" with both his eyes and his pencil. It is important that you stress the fact that the drawings might at first be disconnected, out of proportion, and very disappointing. Explain that this is an excellent way to learn—by making mistakes. You may of course, have a child who does extremely well the first time and poorly the next. Keep on trying until the artist has learned just *why* his first effort was a success or failure. This method is especially valuable for junior-high or high-school youngsters.

As with the development of the tree discussed in the last chapter, you will find some young people are very visually minded and others more emotionally expressive. You should be prepared to stimulate both types. If your child is inclined toward expressionistic artwork, ask questions such as "Why is the figure running? Is he afraid? Is he trying to win a race?" The feelings of the figure will greatly influence the actual rendering.

Other children are more interested in realistic detail, such as the play of light upon the figure or facial features, or a concern with clothes and their folds. To a child who has shown this kind of interest, ask him questions about color, light, etc. He will show a great interest in proportion and faithful representation, while the expressionistic child will probably exaggerate features and colors. In any event, no matter which kind of artist he is, you must encourage him to abandon all stereotyped images of the figure, and if you use the approaches described here, you are bound to succeed.

Illus. 222. Use black tempera, dark crayon, charcoal or India ink for silhouette drawings.

Illus. 223. Memory Drawing. Here the artist studies the model in an action pose. Then the model leaves the stand and the drawing is done from memory. This method is most likely to allow for personal expression, since each artist will undoubtedly have a different "memory" of the pose.

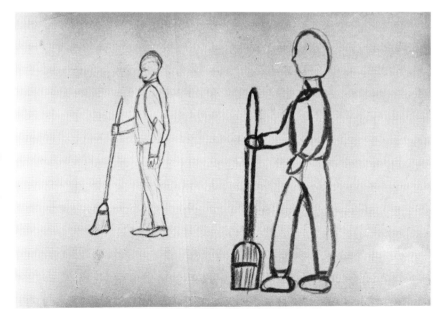

Illus. 224. Soft-tip pens come in a tremendous variety of colors and point widths and can be used to make exceedingly fine detail or large background areas. Here, Milly, grade eleven, beautifully illustrates the exciting decorative effects that can be achieved.

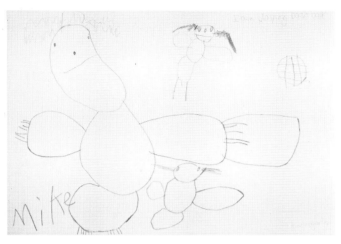

**Illus. 225. Five-year-old Mike uses a large pencil to render his self-portrait entitled "I Am Playing Baseball."**

# CHAPTER THIRTEEN

# Exploring with Media

Media are of great importance in creative art. They are the *tools* which artists use to express their ideas in the best possible way. You may find that one child may be able to express himself most effectively in paint, another in crayon. Still other children find collage or montage the most exciting. As an adult, your task is to help a child make discoveries with the material of his choice, to invent new methods for using media and to investigate the possibilities *and* the limitations of the various materials. In these next chapters, I will discuss the creative use of various materials. Naturally, each medium requires an entire book to be complete, but I hope the suggestions and examples shown will be helpful and will serve as a springboard.

Drawing is considered by most artists to be one of the most basic and elemental techniques but there are many artists who become painters and sculptors without ever learning how to draw. Nevertheless, a small child's first tool is almost always a simple drawing pencil.

For the very young 2½- or 3-year-old, pencils are often safer, because crayons, perhaps because of their delightful color and texture, are occasionally *consumed* rather than used! A large kindergarten pencil and a variety of other pencils ranging from soft to hard will be more inviting to a youngster than a single hard pencil which will limit him in his effects.

Some examples of young children's expression in pencil are shown in Illus. 225 through 228, representing kindergarten age through the fourth grade, and show a progression from simple outlines to shading effects.

The wonderfully imaginative "Landing of the Martians" in Illus. 229 was executed with a flair pen which allowed the young artist to produce his drawing with bold, free, dark lines.

**Illus. 226. Second-grader Sue chose to use pencil to show how she cleans house.**

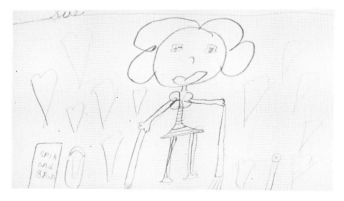

**Illus. 227. Another second-grader, Mike, uses his pencil for shading effects in his drawing "I Am Playing F Troop," inspired by a television series.**

**Illus. 228. "I Am Reading" illustrates Rob, a fourth-grader. The use of the pencil in art never really ends, although most professional artists prefer to do their line drawings in ink.**

Soft-tip pens are becoming more and more popular with artists, teachers and children. The tremendous range of colors and widths of tip that have become available in recent years has expanded their use greatly. Many artists use the big 1- and 2-inch pens for "painting." Therefore, you should investigate the various kinds of pens available.

After a visit to the circus, two 6-year-olds were inspired

Illus. 229. "The Landing of the Martians" is here executed by Mike with a flair pen, a popular medium among artists young and old.

Illus. 230. This time Mike uses soft-tip pens in different colors to produce "I Am in a Racing Car on My Way to California."

to use soft-tip pens to express the brilliant multi-color impressions that they had of the clowns they had seen (Illus. 231 and Illus. 232). As you can see, these pens are useful for lines, dots, or blocks of color. A high-school student produced the powerful figure drawing in Illus. 233 using blue, orange, and brown soft-tip pens which allowed her to effectively convey the solidity and roundness of the figure quickly and easily without having to pause for detail. Compare this with the great detail of Illus. 224 and you will see the tremendous versatility of this medium for expression of all kinds.

Charcoal and conte crayon round out the list of

**Illus. 231. Soft-tip pens are becoming increasingly popular. The many colors of the circus clowns inspired a 6-year-old to use a variety of pens for her clown portrait.**

**Illus. 232. Her friend, another 6-year-old, also felt that soft-tip pens were the best means of capturing the gay quality of a clown.**

Conte crayon produces a soft brown tone, and interesting results are obtained upon different papers having various surfaces. In Illus. 234 a high-schooler has used "mixed media"—charcoal, conte crayon and black India ink—to express her interpretation of the human figure.

Now that we have seen some of the possibilities of drawing materials, let us examine some of the other media in more detail.

**Illus. 234. Here Melissa uses mixed media in her life drawing—charcoal, Conté crayon, and India ink—and has achieved a variety of values and textures.**

**Illus. 233. Melissa, a high-school student, explores the possibilities of soft-tip pens in rendering her figure drawing. She found she was able to capture the pose quickly and effectively.**

drawing tools for children from the late elementary years through high school. Charcoal is available in a variety of stick widths and varying values may be obtained according to the pressure applied and the degree of hardness of the charcoal. Try using charcoal on grey paper and add white crayon for a third value.

CHAPTER FOURTEEN

# Exploring with Crayons and Colored Chalk

### Crayons

Of all the media used by youngsters, crayons are probably the most popular. They are inexpensive and can be purchased almost anywhere. They come in a great variety of hues, shapes and sizes. Their ingredients vary so that a number of different effects can be achieved—dull, pastel and transparent; waxy, shiny, enamel-like; rich surfaces similar to oil painting; tempera-like surfaces. They have the added bonus of leaving little or no mess.

These advantages can, however, be a mixed blessing. Often children become so attached to crayons that they tend to avoid other art materials and thereby limit their own creative expression. You will find that each child has his most suitable medium for expressing his ideas, but he must first be exposed to all the possibilities. Therefore, even when using crayons, children should be consistently motivated to explore, discover and invent new ways of using this common tool. Let's start by examining all the parts of the crayon.

### The Point, End and Side

The three basic parts of the crayon are the point, the broad, peeled side and the blunt end. Using all three parts, a sixth-grader produced the unusual drawing shown in Illus. 235. Have children try out these various effects. The side of the crayon was stroked against the

Illus. 235. The point, the blunt end, and the peeled broad side of a crayon were all used by a sixth-grader to create the unusual effects shown here.

paper to produce the large woven pattern of the basket. The point, side and end were used to create the foliage and blossoms. By swerving the crayon back and forth, the broad side was used to create the wavy leaves.

144

Other parts were made by holding the side of a peeled crayon in the exact middle and rocking the two ends back and forth. Still others were the result of turning the crayon in a complete circle to produce the circular shapes. The blunt end was pressed flat against the paper and the entire crayon was rotated to make some of the smaller parts. Elsewhere, pieces were broken off the end of the crayon to produce jagged edges which were pressed and twisted against the paper.

This drawing was the result of an exciting preliminary exploration into the crayon's effects, as was Illus. 236, also done by a sixth-grader. This young artist chose to create his plant using only the point of his crayons and produced a drawing in the tradition of the Pointillist painters such as Seurat and Signac. These two examples show how one effect can create just as unusual a drawing as a combination of effects. There are so many possibilities that a child is limited only by his own explorations.

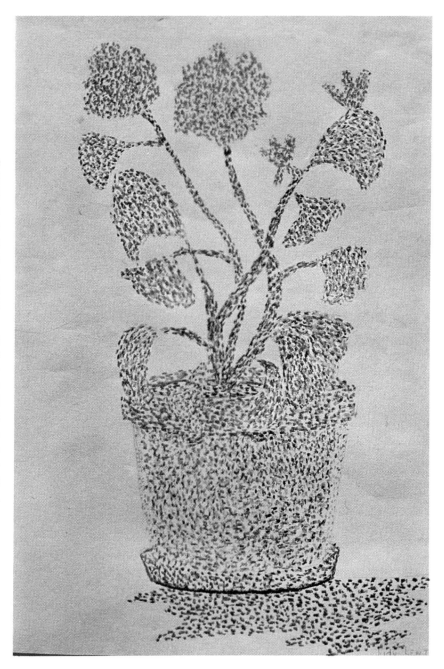

**Illus. 236. Another sixth-grader used only the points of his crayons in the tradition of the great Pointillist painters of the late 19th and early 20th centuries.**

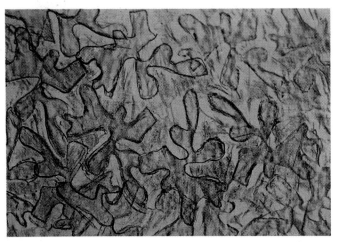

Illus. 237. Crayon relief. An interesting cardboard shape, placed beneath a piece of newsprint in various positions took on this design when the peeled sides of a red crayon were repeatedly rubbed over the newsprint. Grade five.

## Crayon Relief

This technique is the same as rubbing a pencil point over a thin sheet of paper covering a coin until the design shows through. However, using crayons and any number of different materials, exciting patterns and textures will emerge.

Use newsprint for the rubbing paper and manila or construction paper or cardboard to cut out shapes—animals, people, nonrepresentational forms (Illus. 237). When rubbing the broad side over the form which is covered with newsprint the impression is picked up easily. Combine one or two shapes which will introduce the child to the beauty of repeat designs. You will probably discover that the broad side of a *long* crayon creates a more effective impression than that of a short one. If your child's patterns appear to be indistinct, ask him if he thought cutting out his shapes in three or four layers at the same time might help. He will discover that the edges are considerably sharpened up.

Cardboard, tagboard or posterboard can be placed

Illus. 238. Crayon relief. Leaves, embroidery, string, netting, a mesh vegetable bag, and a brick were used to create the separate textures of this collage. Grade ten.

over textured materials such as mesh bags or screens so the newsprint picks up not only the impressions of the objects but the textured background. A child might keep a "texture box" which contains all kinds of things such as sandpaper, burlap, potato sacking, place mats, vegetable graters, etc. Encourage a child to look around his own evironment to discover textured objects. He will start to notice bricks, bathroom tiles, radiator grills, even book covers. All of these surfaces are excellent for relief drawing.

Collages can be created by using individual textures on separate pieces of newsprint and then cutting them into shapes to represent, for example, a person or an animal. Or, a nonrepresentational composition could also be created by the same means.

Experiment with a child of third-grade age and over to discover the principles of design that nonrepresentational art can reveal. Ask such questions as: "How many shapes can you think of that are not circles, squares or triangles? Imagine the shape of a square cracker after you have taken a bite from it. Then another bite, and another. Cut this shape out and see what happens when you over-lap the shape by moving it about at random beneath the newsprint. What happens when the design runs off the edges of the paper?" The child will suddenly realize that he has created *new* shapes. Then have him add another shape on top of this one and still more shapes will appear.

**Illus. 239. Crayon relief. A piece of string was formed into an interesting shape, rubbed with crayon, then the news-print moved slightly and rubbed again. The resulting double image created unusual shapes which were filled in with crayon.**

**Illus. 240. Crayon encaustic. A muffin tin placed on a large can with a 100-watt light bulb inside it will serve to keep the crayons in a molten condition while working.**

The crayon-relief technique is an ideal way for a child to learn the elements of design—repetition of unified shapes, having variety in their repetition—and it's also an exciting technique.

A piece of string is an important object in crayon relief. It can be a line, or it can form shapes. It also provides texture and pattern. Strings can form representational objects or imaginative designs, particularly when used in conjunction with a textured background such as a mesh bag or a screen.

## Crayon Encaustic

Melted wax opens up a whole new avenue for exploration with crayons. Heat makes it possible to paint with this medium, and by varying the amount of heat, the consistency of the liquid can be controlled. Although crayons can be melted over the flame of a burning candle, there is a much safer method. Place peeled crayons in a muffin tin, one color to a compartment. Then either place the muffin tin in a slightly larger tin filled with hot water or put it on top of a large can that has a 100-watt light bulb inside as shown in Illus. 240. Either one will keep the crayons in a molten state for

quite some time, although you will probably have to replace the hot water from time to time. If you wish, you can place the water-filled tin over a very low flame on the stove, but this is inconvenient.

Apply the melted wax with a stiff-bristle brush, tongue depressor or palette knife. Almost any surface can be used—paper, burlap, glass, cardboard, masonite. The encaustic technique can also be used when working with three-dimensional objects. You can even decorate bottles or other sculptured forms.

## Crayon Resist

There are two basic approaches to the crayon-resist technique, which is simply applying a wash over crayon. The first consists of making a crayon drawing in light colors upon light-colored paper and then painting a dark-colored wash over it. The second is exactly the opposite, that is, using dark colors on a sheet of dark construction paper and painting a light-colored wash over it. The aim is to produce brilliant color contrasts.

Manila is a successful paper for this process, but

**Illus. 241. Crayon encaustic. A stiff bristle brush was used to apply molten wax to a black construction paper background. Grade three.**

**Illus. 242. Crayon resist. Here a dark wash has been applied to a light-colored crayon drawing made on light-colored paper. Grade five.**

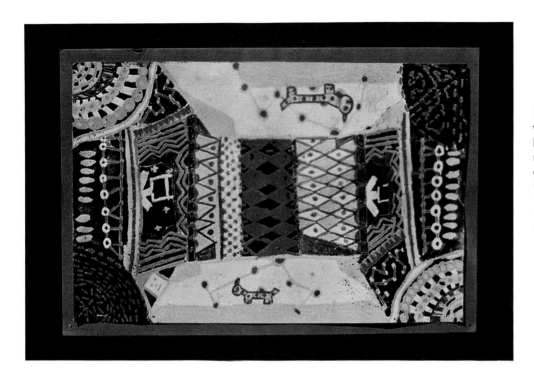

Illus. 243. Crayon resist. The wax lines must be applied heavily to the paper. Be careful not to use a color on your drawing that is identical to the wash you intend to apply. You can leave uncolored areas that will then be covered by the wash. Grade five.

Illus. 244. Crayon resist. A fascinating crayon design such as this is enhanced when a brilliant wash is applied. Grade five.

Illus. 245. Crayon resist. Here, a light wash was applied to a dark-colored drawing on dark paper, producing a completely different effect from the previous examples. Grade twelve.

Illus. 246. Crayon etching. The application of etchings to containers such as milk cartons, oatmeal cartons, and coffee cans turns such cast-offs into decorative and useful objects. The paper design should be stapled to the container and a coat of clear shellac applied. Grade five.

colored construction paper also provides interesting effects. Tagboard, being hard and smooth, produces a bolder and sharper effect since the surface is less porous than manila paper. Therefore the crayon markings are less likely to get lost beneath the wash. Also, the wax builds up more easily on the surface and the artist does not have to press his crayon as hard to achieve a heavy line. Shelf paper, brown wrapping paper, and wallpaper can also be used with interesting results. Even a sheet of newspaper containing fine print can be used. (The lines of print provide a guide for creating patterns, but the printed matter disappears once the wash has been added.) The wash can be tempera paint mixed to the consistency of thin cream, but many children will want to experiment with various hues of transparent water color to expand upon the range of effects.

The crayon-resist technique will allow children to express their ideas in a bold, free, and colorful way, whether they are creating representational (Illus. 245) or nonrepresentational designs.

## Crayon Etching

This is another simple technique, but it too produces striking and unusual results. The entire surface of a sheet of tagboard is covered with a layer of crayon, either of one color or many colors laid on in a random fashion. Then a black wash of India ink, tempera (add soap), marker ink, or crayon is painted over the surface and allowed to dry completely. A sharp tool such as a lead pencil is used to etch a design into the dark surface, but you must be very careful not to damage the crayon surface. If a child has difficulty covering the crayon with ink or tempera, pat a chalk eraser containing chalk dust on the crayoned surface just before adding the ink.

There are many possible tools that can be used for etching. Have the child experiment with such things as a hair comb or a fork to achieve evenly spaced flowing lines; the blunt end of a needle, the point of a nail or nail file to etch lines of varying width; a paring knife or razor blade (single-edge) to remove large areas of ink.

Illus. 247. An imaginative use of the crayon-etching technique has been employed here by a sixth-grader who chose it to portray fields as seen through the window of a helicopter high up in the sky.

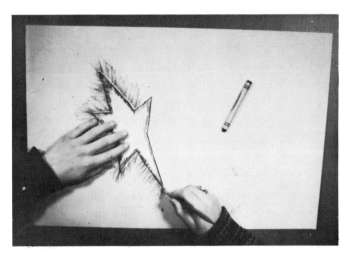

Illus. 249. Place Stencil A upon a large sheet of paper after rubbing the edges thoroughly with crayon. Then brush and streak the color from the stencil onto the paper. Repeat this process until you have a design that suits you. Grade three.

Illus. 248. The crayon-stencil technique provides young artists with an excellent means of exploring certain design concepts. Here a third-grader cuts an interesting shape from a piece of tagboard. The cut-out star is Stencil A, the hole in the tagboard will be Stencil B.

Illus. 250. To achieve a reverse design, use Stencil B and rub crayon thoroughly around the edges of the hole, place it on a paper and rub toward the hole. Grade three.

## Crayon-Stencil Technique

This is an ideal technique for children in the third-grade to sixth-grade age group because it provides an avenue leading directly to a concept of repetition of shape, design and color. Most people think of repetition as being boring and monotonous, but when it is used to create multitudes of original designs, they suddenly realize its possibilities.

To begin, have the child cut out a shape of his choice, preferably from tagboard because it does not tear easily. This shape will be called Stencil A and is shown at the bottom of Illus. 248. The hole left in the paper (top of Illus. 248) will be Stencil B. Rub crayon around the edges of Stencil A and place it on a large sheet of paper. Then brush and streak the color from the shape onto the paper. A pencil eraser, finger or tissue all work very well for this process. Be sure to rub in one direction only— *away from* the stencil. After the shape is completely transferred, lift it, apply another coat of crayon to the edges and lay it down in a different area of the paper. Repeat this process until satisfied with the design. The shapes can be overlapped as shown in Illus. 251. Notice how this fourth-grade artist combined his finished stencil pattern with the crayon-relief technique in Illus. 252.

Now, with Stencil B you can add a reverse design to your paper. Place it over the positive design and apply crayon to the edges. Then rub the crayon *toward the open area*. Notice that the shape is the same, but the streaks of color now radiate toward the middle of each stencilled shape. The completed composition will show a very different pattern from the original star—many new shapes and linear patterns will be formed by overlapping and varying the stencil effect.

An even greater variety can be achieved by using several different colors.

**Illus. 251. An overlapping design has been created here with Stencil B.**

**Illus. 252. The same design combined with the crayon-relief technique. Newsprint was placed over a mesh vegetable bag to create texture in certain areas of the design. Grade three.**

## Colored Chalk

One of the least expensive mediums, chalk comes in a wide variety of hues in boxes of as few as eight sticks or as many as 100. Two varieties are available—soft chalk which is made from alabaster and which is very inexpensive, and dustless chalk which is harder and also nonallergenic.

## Blending Colors

Colors are very easily blended. If, for instance, a child were making an early evening sky or a sunrise, he could use blue, purple, white, yellow and orange, and, with a facial tissue or his fingertips, rub and blend the colors into a single mass of subtle tones. All kinds of shading can be accomplished the same way.

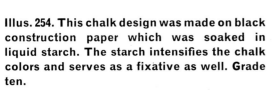

**Illus. 253. This design was achieved by applying colored chalk to blue paper which was soaked in sugar-water. Grade twelve.**

**Illus. 254. This chalk design was made on black construction paper which was soaked in liquid starch. The starch intensifies the chalk colors and serves as a fixative as well. Grade ten.**

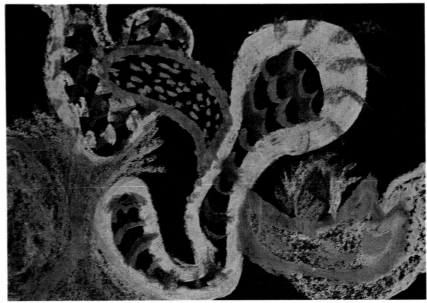

154

Illus. 255. The stencil technique can be used with chalk in the same way as with crayon. Both Stencils A and B created this unified, rhythmic design. Grade five.

## Chalk over Powdered Paint

Magnificent results can be achieved when chalk is used with white powdered paint. Soak a sheet of paper, plain or colored, in water. Remove and sprinkle a tablespoonful of white powdered paint on the paper. Use paper at least 12 × 18 inches in size for the best effects. Blend the white powdered paint over the wet paper. While the paint is still wet, but not flooded, take a stick of colored chalk and, using the long side, push it around the paper. Then, use another color. A beautiful blend of colors will result. When dry, the colors will not rub off, as the white powdered paint acts as a fixative.

## Drawing on Moistened Paper

There are several moistening agents that can be used. If you soak the paper with a water-soaked cloth or sponge, you can add sugar to the water to serve as a fixative. Water-soaked paper will produce flowing chalk lines, masses and shapes, and will also eliminate chalk dust. Encourage children to experiment with a variety of strokes, lines and patterns and to mix and blend their colors directly on the paper. The chalk can be treated almost as though it were paint. After applying the chalk use a brush to swirl it around, or make designs such as in Illus. 253.

Another agent is milk—regular, powdered milk and water, or buttermilk. Like sugar-water it acts as a fixative. Try brushing the milk on the paper (which should be placed on a damp newspaper in order to retard the drying process) and then applying the chalk. Or dip the chalk sticks in the milk and apply to dry paper. Dried milk can be removed easily from the chalk tips by rubbing the sticks on a rough surface. Another method is

155

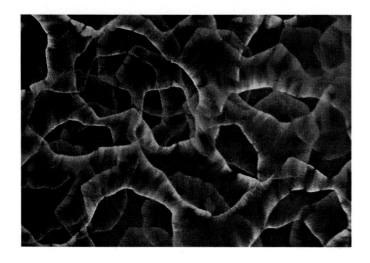

Illus. 256. Interesting effects can be achieved by using light-colored chalk on dark paper. Grade five.

Illus. 257. The reverse—dark—colored chalk on light paper produced this unusual design. Grade five.

to spray a watery solution of powdered milk on the chalk drawing.

A mixture of one-part liquid starch and one-part water was used in Illus. 254 to moisten the paper before the chalk design was added. This mixture also provides an excellent, inexpensive fixative when sprayed on finished chalk drawings. Use an atomizer or insecticide sprayer.

As with crayon, the stencil technique (page 153) can be used with chalk. Both Stencils A and B produced the unusual rhythmic design in Illus. 255, done by a fifth-grader.

**Illus. 258. (Photo courtesy of Binney and Smith, Inc.)**

CHAPTER FIFTEEN

# Exploring with Paints

There are several different kinds of paint that are available—tempera, water color, casein, oil, and acrylic. However, tempera paint, also called poster paint and show-card paint, is the most popular painting medium for young people. It is inexpensive, dries quickly, is odorless and the colors are opaque. Therefore, although I will discuss the other paints, our major explorations will be with tempera.

## Tempera

Tempera is available in liquid form or as a powder. The powder must be mixed with water, of course, but it is somewhat less expensive than the liquid.

## Mixing

Powdered tempera and water should be mixed to the consistency of light cream. The paint should be thin enough to flow easily from the brush and thick enough so that colors are truly opaque when applied to newsprint. Too-thin tempera is impossible to use when working on an easel—it will drip uncontrollably.

When mixing, place the powder in a jar first. Little by little add water, at the same time stirring with a spoon or tongue depressor. Never add the powder to water because you will find it is too difficult to judge the proportions and you will end up with far too much paint by the time you have reached the proper consistency. If possible, mix the powder and water at least twenty-four hours before using because the pigments need sufficient time to absorb the moisture. When first mixed, the paint is grainy looking, and sandlike lumps will appear on the paper. You will find that after twenty-four hours some of the colors will have thickened to mud consistency because powders differ in their absorbing powers. However, water can be added easily when necessary.

If a powder has a tendency to float on the water no matter how hard you stir, add a tablespoon of dry or liquid detergent. Use an egg beater to mix the tempera, water and detergent. Detergent also makes painting on surfaces that are slightly waxy much easier. (Do not add detergent to tempera that is to be used in crayon resist.)

There will be times when you want to mix tempera for immediate use, and there are three quick-and-easy methods:

(1) *Flour-on-water.* Pour water in a clean jar with a lid, using half as much water as the paint needed. Pour an equal amount of dry powder into the jar, cover, and shake vigorously until thoroughly mixed. Test on paper, and add water to thin, and powder to thicken as needed.

Illus. 259. Messy paint trays or cups are not needed when paint is mixed directly on paper. The "direct" mixing approach resulted in the blended colors and various textures in this tenth-grader's "Farm Work."

(2) *Dry palette*. This method is clean and economical. Shake very small piles of powder onto a tinfoil-lined cookie sheet or tinfoil plate. Dip your brush first into water and then into the powder. When you apply it to the paper you are actually mixing it at the same time.

(3) *Sprinkle*. This is especially useful for large areas such as background colors. Using a sponge, apply clear water to the paper. Sift the powder lightly before using in order to avoid lumps and then sprinkle it onto the moistened paper. Blend with your brush.

Unlike liquid tempera, some powdered tempera paints do not contain a preservative. Once mixed with water, stored paint will begin to spoil within a few days, causing a disagreeable odor. A teaspoonful of oil of wintergreen will cause the liquefied powder to remain sweet for months, or even years.

Smear vaseline or cold cream around the inner rim of each paint bottle and cover before the colors are stored, making it easier to remove the lids later on.

## Brushes

Bristle brushes are best for the young child—kindergarten through third grade. Hair brushes can be used from the fourth grade on. The older child has greater concern for detail and the hair brush is better adapted for this purpose.

One of the great problems in painting is preserving true colors if a single paint brush is used. Light colors such as white and yellow turn muddy when traces of dark paint are left by an uncleaned brush. Older children can generally be depended upon to dip their brushes in

158

clear water when changing from one color to another. With younger children you might teach them to use brushes that are saved only for a single color. The "red brush" is always kept in the red paint jar throughout the painting session, the "green brush" in the green jar, and so on.

Be sure that paint brushes are washed in warm water and soap after use. They should be stored upside down, bristle up, in bottles or cans so that the bristles do not become permanently bent over.

## Brayers

A printing brayer is a handy instrument for applying tempera to a large surface such as mural backgrounds. Roll the tempera out onto a flat surface such as a cookie sheet or aluminium foil so that the paint is even in consistency. When the brayer is covered with paint of a fairly smooth texture, apply to the paper. Then you can use a brush to add details or to accent large shapes and forms.

## Papers

Newsprint, manila paper and white drawing paper are commonly used with tempera. Manila paper is especially popular because its rough texture permits the artist to create both rough and smooth brush strokes. Newsprint has the smoothest surface and is the least expensive.

## Permanent Surfaces

Tempera surfaces are not permanent. Pigments easily rub off when paintings are handled excessively. You can mix library paste into liquid tempera which will preserve the surface to some extent. Shellac, clear varnish or lacquer may also be applied over the tempera surface but they tend to darken the surface as well as adding a gloss which may or may not be desirable. The best solution is to use a commercial fixative or hair spray which will not affect the surface nor darken it. Use sparingly; that is, do not overspray. Two thin coats are recommended.

**Illus. 260. Fresh, spontaneous effects and subtle gradations of tone can occur when you use the direct mixing method. Notice the interesting brush strokes in this painting by a twelfth-grader.**

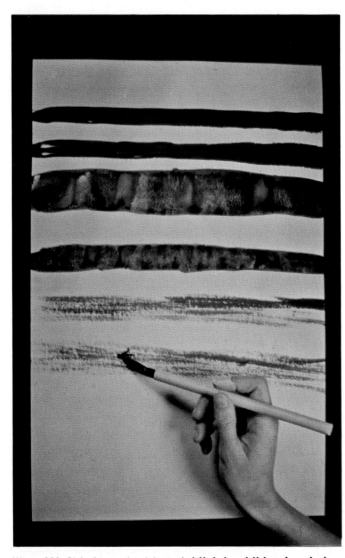

**Illus. 261.** It is important to establish in children's minds the difference between opaque and transparent colors and the fact that paints can be lightened and darkened by varying the water content. It is not always necessary to add white or black paint to lighten or darken colors.

## Experimenting with Color

When your child is all set up with tempera paints and brush or brushes, you might start by getting him interested in opaque and transparent color effects. Ask questions such as "What happens when you make a line with a brush that is loaded with paint (Illus. 261, top)? How would you describe this line? Can you see through it?" The answer will probably be "It's a dark line. I can't see through it." Then identify this line as being *opaque*.

"Now use a large amount of water and very little paint. What happens now? How is this line different from the opaque line?" The child will notice that now the color is light and he can see through it. Identify this line then as being *transparent*. Ask "When might you use a watery, thin, transparent color? For ocean, sky? How about the dark opaque line? For objects on the ocean or the sky?"

This little experiment shows a child that he need not add white or black paint to lighten or darken his temperas. He can do either by varying the water content. At the same time you have established in his mind the difference between opaque and transparent colors.

## Exploring with Texture

"Let's make a line with a brush that is almost dry (Illus. 261, bottom two lines). Just put the paint on the end of your brush and do not add water. How would you describe this line?" "It's rough." "What does this line remind you of?" "A tree trunk. A rock. Bricks." "Can you think of other ways to create pattern and texture with your brush?"

Illus. 262 shows how one child created a stippled effect by using the tip of her brush (right). Then she made a completely different pattern by using the side of her brush (left). Illus. 263 shows how a ninth-grader put her new-found knowledge to work. She created the painting "On the Phone" by using the stippled effect for the entire picture. Through the use of lights and darks, the young artist has suggested shading and by using darks on the edges has created a three-dimensional effect.

Another exciting method for creating texture is painting on tissue paper. Crumple a piece of white tissue paper, and with library paste apply it to a piece of manila paper. Let it dry, and run a paint-loaded brush over the tissue and you will discover only the raised areas of the tissue pick up the paint (Illus. 264). You might try soaking the crumpled tissue in clear water first—you will discover that the effect is similar but softer looking.

Illus. 265, painted by a sixth-grader, illustrates the use of the crumpled-tissue effect. This child has pasted tissue down and painted it to create texture for the trees, bushes and roof of the house. Notice how this adds interest to the entire painting by contrasting the smooth and the rough, the light and the dark.

An unusual seascape is shown in Illus. 266, done by a twelfth-grader who tried something a little different. She painted her crumpled tissue dark blue, making sure both the raised and recessed areas were filled with color. When dry, she brushed a light blue color over the dark

**Illus. 262. The point and sides of the brush can be used to create different textures and patterns.**

**Illus. 263. Here a ninth-grader has used the stippling effect to make her entire painting, "On the Phone."**

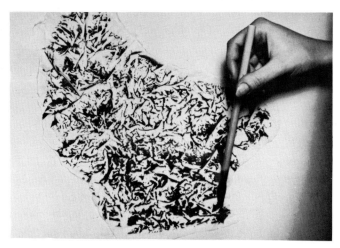

**Illus. 264. Crumpled tissue paper, pasted to manila paper, produces an interesting texture when tempera is painted across the rough surface.**

blue tissue, covering only the raised areas, and the result suggests splashing, swirling ocean waves on a windy day. The sky, surrounding water and the sailboats are painted directly on the manila paper.

A synthetic or natural sponge is a versatile tool for applying tempera paint. Have your child experiment with a sponge to discover the variety of effects that are possible. For example, a dry sponge dipped into tempera will produce a lacy, spotted, textural effect while a water-soaked sponge dipped in tempera produces a smoother look. Have the child use a paint-loaded sponge on dry paper and then on water-soaked paper. Bleeding can be achieved when a paint-loaded sponge is applied to a sheet of water-soaked manila paper. Illus. 267 shows the texture created by using the *end* of a dry synthetic

**Illus. 265. "Our Home" shows the use of the crumpled-tissue-paper technique to make rough textures in the trees, roof and bushes. Grade six.**

162

**Illus. 266.** A twelfth-grader created a striking seascape using crushed tissue to suggest the turbulent waves.

sponge dipped in tempera, while Illus. 268 is an example of how a ninth-grader used a natural sponge to produce the lacy open foliage of the trees and the grassy areas beyond the brick fence.

What other materials could make interesting textural patterns on paper? In Illus. 269, a crumpled piece of paper dipped in tempera produces a unique pattern when applied with varying pressures to the paper. In Illus. 270, a fifth-grader uses a tightly crumpled piece of paper dipped in tempera to achieve an unusual delicate texture in his painting "Chick-a-wat-sis." You might try many other materials, such as cloths of different textures—from silk to burlap.

**Illus. 267.** The end of a dry synthetic sponge dipped into paint produces unusual textural effects.

Illus. 268. "House at Night," painted by a ninth-grader. Here a natural sponge dipped in paint created the unusual lacy effect of the trees and grass, adding to the eerie atmosphere of the scene.

Illus. 269. There are many "tools" that you can use for textural patterns. Even a piece of crumpled paper dipped in paint is an effective pattern-maker, as you can see.

Illus. 270. The delicate, light-blue texture in the upper part of a fifth-grader's painting, "Chick-a-wat-sis," was made with crumpled paper dipped in tempera.

## Wet Technique

"Let's try soaking our paper to see what happens when we add color. First make a line on the top of the paper (Illus. 271). Now soak the bottom of the paper with clear water. Paint a line through it. What has happened?" "It flows." "It makes patterns." "Paint a picture using the wet technique. First, think of all the things that it would be best suited for."

"Walking in the Rain" (Illus. 272) done by a fourth-grader, uses the wet technique to great effect. This child began by soaking her paper and adding greys and reds, which to her represented the atmosphere of a rainy day. Then she drew in her figures and the house and tree with black crayon when the paper was dry. She very successfully conveyed the feeling of rain without actually showing it realistically as she might have with puddles or raindrops.

In "The Lighthouse" (Illus. 274), a fifth-grader has

Illus. 271. You have seen how a dry brush produces rough textural effects. Now add water to achieve the opposite result—smooth, flowing colors.

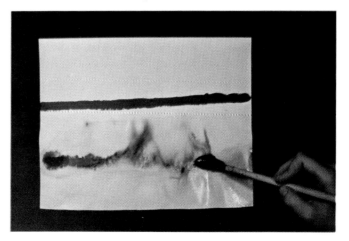

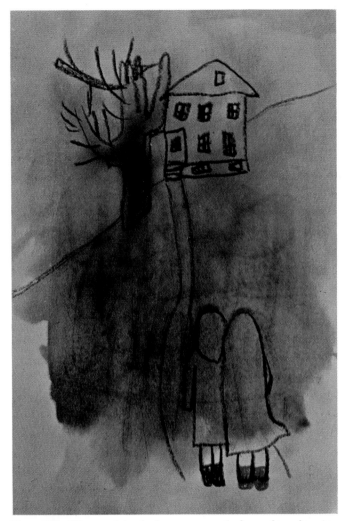

effectively combined the wet technique and the dry-brush technique. He began by soaking his sheet of manila paper in a pail of clear water. Then he placed the water-soaked paper onto a newspaper and dabbled black tempera into the sky area to create soft clouds. He tilted the newspaper and the painting so that the black paint would flow and bleed horizontally. He was very careful not to let it enter the lower half of the paper. Then he let it dry. Using a dry brush and black tempera, he painted in the silhouettes of the lighthouse, cliff, tree and the sailboat at anchor.

The wet technique is excellent for blending colors. Paint two colors onto the water-soaked paper and tilt and you will have a new third color! Keep a child experimenting with this technique until he sees the range of possibilities.

Colors can be blended on a sheet of dry paper by mixing the colors on a paint brush. By dipping the brush all of the way into the blue paint jar, then halfway into the jar of white paint, one young artist used the side of her dual-colored brush to create the blue and white flower pattern in Illus. 273.

**Illus. 272. The wet technique suggested a rainy day to one fourth-grader who, after painting her water-soaked paper, used a dark crayon to add a house, a tree, and two people in raincoats "Walking in the Rain."**

**Illus. 273. These unique daisies are being created by a young artist who discovered that she can blend colors on dry paper by dipping her brush all the way into one jar of paint and halfway into another.**

Illus. 274. This unusual effect was created by combining the wet and dry techniques. Grade five.

## Mixing New Colors

Young children use their colors primarily to express themselves—their ideas or their moods. If left alone, children will select, not representational colors, but expressionistic ones. If a child loves pure colors, let him use them to his heart's content but very often he will make his own discoveries by accident.

Children from the fourth-grade level up through high school should be encouraged to mix their tempera as much as possible. They will learn a great deal about the complex science of color through experience. They are bound to get excited about the possibilities of mixed color and this is when you should introduce to them the basic elements of color terminology and theory.

The color wheel in Illus. 276 shows the *primary* and *secondary* colors. Red, yellow and blue are the primaries, which, when two are mixed together, create the secondaries. The primary colors red and yellow produce the secondary color orange; yellow and blue make green; blue and red produce purple. Three primary colors mixed together create *tertiary* colors—as when red, yellow, and blue are mixed, they produce the tertiary color brown. Colors straight from the jar are called *pure* colors. A *tint* is made by adding white paint to a pure color and a *shade* is created by adding black paint to a pure color. A *tone* is the result of mixing black and white with a pure color.

167

Illus. 275. The light, airy feeling of this fourth-grader's painting, "Springtime," was achieved by using mixed colors only. Children should be encouraged to experiment with mixing and blending as much as possible.

Illus. 276. The color wheel.

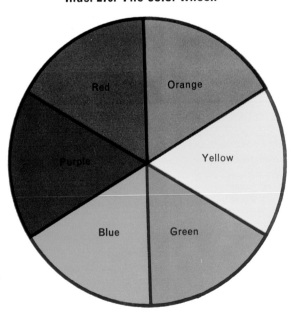

## Line Painting with Tempera

Line paintings are fun and challenging to young artists. You should encourage a child to experiment as much as he likes with lines. It is an excellent way to learn to handle a brush as well as to discover the potential of the brush. Thick, thin, opaque and transparent colors should be used.

Begin by suggesting a series of lines such as shown in Illus. 277. Try to make the child conscious of the brush and how it feels when making different kinds of lines. For example, a thin line requires a light touch, a thick line requires a certain amount of pressure. Then a thick-thin line requires a light and a heavy touch. Ask how it feels when he makes a scalloped line or a jagged line. Ask how many different kinds of lines he can think of, how many different kinds of patterns or textures can be made with lines. Encourage him to make free designs such as shown in Illus. 278 through 279. Suggest other

**Illus. 277. Line Painting. (1) is a thin line created by holding the brush lightly and moving it swiftly across the paper. By pressing harder upon the brush, a thicker line is made (2). A wavy line (3) is achieved by varying the pressure on the brush—heavy, light, heavy. Move the brush up and down to make scallops and curves (4), or use the side of the brush to make short fat lines (5).**

kinds of line paintings such as animals, insects, or whatever else he chooses. With each experiment he will become more and more skillful.

## Water Colors

Water colors have both advantages and disadvantages for young children. Their best quality is their lovely, transparent and delicate hue. Also, clean-up involves very little work. A wet brush will clean the areas around the cakes and the brushes can be quickly washed.

The main disadvantage with water colors is that they are difficult to control. Because they are thin and transparent, a painting must really be carefully planned. They are not easy to correct—overpainting is almost impossible and young children become frustrated when they cannot cover their mistakes. They can, however, be made more controllable by using liquid starch as a moistening medium in place of water. The starch adds body to the paint but it does not create opacity.

Water colors are available in cakes, tubes and powders. Cakes are the least expensive and the least complicated to use and are, therefore, the most popular for general use.

Junior-high schoolers should begin using water colors on inexpensive newsprint or shelving paper. High-school-age boys and girls can experiment on water-color papers which come in many sizes, types and weights. The lighter the weight, the less the cost, but the heavier weights provide greater absorbent qualities and allow for richer textural effects.

Always stretch water-color papers before using. Soak a sheet in a tub of water for half an hour at least. Then, with gummed paper tape, attach all sides of the paper to a piece of masonite or plywood which is slightly larger than the paper. Allow to dry completely. Do not remove the paper from the backing until the painting is finished and the water colors have dried.

Experiment with the paint on dry paper to achieve hard-edged strokes. Or soak the water-color paper with a water and sponge, and you will produce free-flowing

Illus. 278. Line paintings can be very beautiful as this fifth-grader's work shows. Notice how all of her lines run off the paper.

Illus. 279. Another fifth-grader has produced a totally different line painting by wiggling his brush back and forth.

effects. The color will bleed into the surface of the paper, creating patterns of a rich hue. Both hair brushes and sponges can be used to achieve textural effects. A razor blade can be used to scratch in white highlights. Using India ink, line can be added to accent certain shapes and to define areas of color as a ninth-grade artist did in "Sunday Afternoon" (Illus. 280).

## Casein

Casein paint is a recent addition to painting media. Casein is a substance found in curdled milk which is commercially mixed with color pigments. Available in both tubes or jars, these paints are mixed with water to create transparent or opaque colors according to the amount of water used. They dry rapidly and produce surfaces that are not as shiny as oil paints. The surface is closer to that of tempera, but unlike tempera, casein produces a permanent and waterproof finish.

## Oils

High-school-age boys and girls will enjoy working with the traditional oil paints. The colors are intense and brilliant, mistakes are easily covered, and thin transparent washes can be combined with rich impastos. A series of washes (oils thinned in linseed oil or turpentine) allows the young artist to achieve transparent, vibrant, shiny areas. Oils straight from the tube can be applied with a palette knife when rough, textural surfaces are desired.

Canvas is the most popular surface for oil painting. It comes in a variety of weights and weaves and can be purchased by the yard. It should be stretched over a wooden frame and tacked in place. However, pre-stretched canvas is available in many art supply stores. Raw canvas should be sized with rabbit-skin glue and painted with white lead before oil is applied. There is also a synthetic canvas available. This is a cardboard with a textured plastic coating.

You might suggest experimenting with oils on either the smooth or the rough side of masonite. Masonite should be covered with a ground coat (which has dried thoroughly) before applying oils.

Illus. 280. Water colors allow older children and adults to produce intense, flowing, transparent areas of color. Here, a ninth-grader used India ink to define shapes and outlines on his water-color painting, "Sunday Afternoon."

## Acrylics

The newest addition to the family of paints is a "plastic paint," composed of acrylic polymer mixed with pigments. Acrylics are applied with water just as are cascin paints, water colors and tempera. They can be mixed to a thin transparent wash or used as thick, opaque impastos up to $\frac{3}{4}$-inch thick.

They have rightfully made a sensation in the art world. Professionals, amateurs, teachers, children are unanimous in their approval of these paints. They dry rapidly and become waterproof immediately. They can be used on a wide variety of surfaces—canvas, masonite, cloth, concrete, plywood, paper, and so on. Surfaces can be matte, semi-matte or glossy. Shiny and/or dull effects can be controlled by adding a special liquid medium.

Pastes and extenders may be added when working in impasto. Any thickness, any texture may be achieved. Young children enjoy the fact that they can cover their mistakes so easily. Acrylics blend beautifully. The painted surface remains flexible. Cracks and peeling do not occur when a painting is tightly rolled. The paints themselves are odorless and fadeproof. Brushes are easily cleaned in soap and water. In every way, these paints are the perfect medium for boys and girls from seventh-grade age up. Make sure that your child is introduced to them. He will be able to do anything with acrylics that he can do with any of the other paints, plus a whole lot more!

**Illus. 281. A colorful bird was conceived by a fifth-grader who had a supply of materials and papers such as wallpaper, newspaper, pieces of cloth, toothpicks, and even** tufts of dog hair left over from a clipping. This is a fine example of imaginative use of scrap which everybody has at hand.

CHAPTER SIXTEEN

# Exploring with Scrap

Although most art topics usually suggest the media to the artist, let's reverse the procedure with scrap materials. Let's start with the scrap and let *it* suggest the topic or subject.

There are four basic classifications for scrap; (1) background materials; (2) applied materials; (3) three-dimensional materials suitable for making such things as masks, puppets, etc.; (4) joining or connecting materials.

See if you can expand upon my lists which follow:

*Background Materials:* Aluminium foil, bottles, burlap, canvas, cardboard (corrugated), cartons, containers, felt, flannel, glass, jars, linoleum, masonite, metallic paper, mirrors, oilcloth, paper plates, pie plates, tin cans, tinfoil, wallboard, wrapping paper.

*Applied Materials:* Acorns, beads, berries, bottles (broken), bottle caps, balsa wood, buckles, buttons, burlap pieces, canvas pieces, carpet wool, cellulose, cellophane, clock parts, Christmas snow, tinsel and icicles, confetti, cord, corn, costume jewelry, cotton batting, cotton swabs, dried leaves, egg shells, excelsior, feathers, felt pieces, film strips, flannel pieces, fluted bonbon cups, fur, glass, ice-cream sticks, inner tubes, jars (broken), lace, leather, linoleum, lollipop sticks, macaroni, magazines (cut and torn), marbles, matchsticks, metallic papers, nails, netting, oilcloth, paper and plastic doilies, pine needles and cones, pipe cleaners, pods, popsicle sticks, reeds, ribbon, rickrack, rings, rice, rope, rug yarn, sand (sprinkled on glue or paste), sandpaper,

Illus. 282. Two fifth-graders are busy putting their scrap materials together to make collage portraits.

Illus. 283. This fifth-grader is proudly showing a classmate his collage which is made up of scrap pieces of sponge rubber and felt appliqued to a paper background. (Photo by John Agee, Los Alamos, New Mexico.)

sea shells, seed pods, seeds, sequins, spaghetti, sponges (bits of), stones, string, tacks, tiles, tinfoil, tissue paper, tongue depressors, toothpicks, twine, vegetable sacks, wallpaper, veiling, wood scraps, wood shavings, wooden beads, wooden blocks, wrapping paper and yarn.

*Three-dimensional Materials:* Aluminium foil (cut, folded), bailing wire, bell wire, bottles, boxes, cardboard rollers, cardboard (corrugated), coat hangers, containers, copper foil (cut, bent), corks, corn husks, driftwood, egg cartons, flash bulbs, gourds, hatboxes, ice-cream sticks, lollipop sticks, mailing tubes, matchsticks (for matchstick sculpture), metal foil (cut, bent), milk containers, paper bags, paper cups, paper tubes, pie plates, pine cones, pipe cleaners, plastic tubing called "spaghetti," popsicle sticks, reeds, soap, socks (for puppets), spools, stockings, stovepipe wire, straws, tin cans, tongue depressors, toothpicks, TV dinner plates, wire, wire mesh, wood scraps, wooden blocks.

*Joining and Connecting Materials:* Bailing wire, bell wire, bobby pins, brass paper fasteners, flour paste,

Illus. 284. Very young children enjoy working with odd bits and pieces of colored papers of various textures to create collages such as this nursery-school boy did.

174

liquid glue, paper clips, rubber bands, rubber cement, stovepipe wire, staples, string, tacks, tape (transparent, masking, adhesive, etc.), thread, twine, wallpaper paste, wheat paste, white library paste, yarn.

## Collage

Collage or "texture pictures," are fun to assemble. The process of creating them increases a child's sensitivity to texture, color and form. In addition, the process of collecting a myriad of objects opens a child's eyes to the value of small or discarded articles. Today, when so many objects become "junk" almost immediately and are not reuseable, such as milk and egg cartons, wrapping paper, etc., it is important to make a child aware of their possibilities in his own personal environment.

Instead of throwing away a used pop bottle or a candy wrapper, he will be able to stow it away in his scrap box. Each kind of material might have its own shopping bag as a storehouse and be labelled "Paper," "Glass," "Wood," and so on. Be sure, however, to encourage a child to rinse out sticky bottles and other containers before putting them away.

**Illus. 285. This texture picture is composed of construction-paper cut-outs and heavy yarn.**

**Illus. 286. Here is a three-dimensional scrap house constructed by a fifth-grader from colored paper, strips of ribbon, Christmas glitter, cotton batting, and aluminium foil.**

**Illus. 287.** Shiny metallic tinfoil suggested an imaginary spaceman to one sixth-grader. Pieces of red and black cloth, yarn, rug filler, buttons and pipe cleaners make up his outfit.

**Illus. 288.** Another sixth-grader had a supply of odd bits of material which immediately conjured up in his mind a hobo. After drawing the figure with a soft-tip pen, he glued on the various pieces of clothing.

If the materials are to suggest a theme or topic, one idea is to join in with the child in making an interesting display of his collection so that everything is on view

at once. Have the child *feel* the materials as well as look at them. Then ask such questions as: "Does this rough piece of burlap suggest a certain kind of person

to you? A lumberjack? How about the lace or the doilies? Does the fur make you think of a certain animal? The feathers? Can you think of anything that you might use *all* of these objects to make? An out-of-doors scene, perhaps?"

Once a child gets the idea, he will start to see all kinds of possibilities—some representational, some imaginary, some nonrepresentational. Illus. 286 through Illus. 295

Illus. 289. Pieces of scrap leather brought to mind a cowgirl, and a sixth-grade artist constructed a collage figure with yarn hair and pieces of rickrack, cord, cotton batting and Christmas glitter for trimmings.

Illus. 290. "Roaring Twenties' Maybelle" is a fifth-grader's rendering of a lady of that period dressed in black yarn hair and various pieces of costume jewelry.

**Illus. 291. "The Hippy." Grade five.**

**Illus. 292. "Dressed in Fur." Grade five.**

show the results of using materials at hand to create collages. These are excellent examples. For instance, crumpled tinfoil immediately conjured up the robotlike figure in Illus. 287 in the sixth-grade artist's mind, and the patches and scraps of material in Illus. 288 produced a travelling hobo, created by another sixth-grader.

A pair of very modish people are shown in Illus. 291 and Illus. 292. Odd bits of fur stimulated a sixth-grader to portray herself in "Dressed in Fur," while fur pieces of another kind produced "The Hippy" in Illus. 291. Bushy hair and a beard were his mental image, and this made him think of a current trend in styles.

Two very different imaginary creatures are shown in

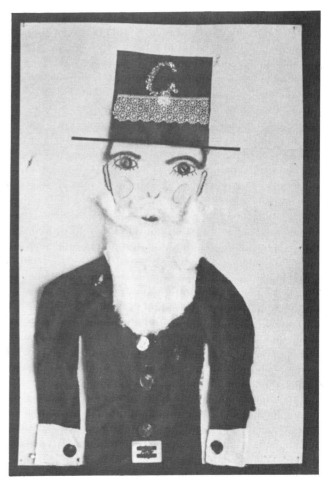

**Illus. 293. "Mother, Ready for Church." Grade five.**

**Illus. 294. "Rip Van Winkle." Grade five.**

Illus. 281 and Illus. 295. Cloth, cotton batting, toothpicks, and wisps of dog's hair (rescued after a grooming session), make up the colorful creature in Illus. 281, done by a fifth-grader, while a third-grader constructed an equally fanciful animal from cloth, yarn, rug filler, and a feather (Illus. 295).

## Mosaics

Any number of materials are suitable for mosaics. Seeds provide a very suitable ingredient, as well as rice or corn, wheat, barley, oats, etc. Soaked in various food colorings, the seeds become even more interesting. Some seeds provide their own natural color, such as watermelon seeds. Young children generally prefer to work with materials that are not too small, and since their attention span dwindles if the work is too detailed, try large pieces of dry breakfast cereal.

Illus. 296. Masonite serves as the background for a tenth-grader's mosaic. Gravel, crushed glass, aquarium gravel, black marbles, and wild rice were glued onto the masonite. Parts of the bird were painted with enamel.

**Illus. 297. Colored aquarium gravel and black yarn are here glued to cardboard to suggest an underwater scene. Grade twelve.**

Eggshells provide a very interesting texture and food colorings can also be applied to them. Pebbles, colored glass, buttons, macaroni (painted with tempera) and wood scraps and shavings are all excellent materials for mosaics. Small pieces of paper of any kind—newspaper, construction paper, tissue, cellophane, crepe—can be torn

**Illus. 298. Cardboard cartons of all kinds can be put together to make any number of objects. This incredible creature has two oatmeal cartons serving as his body and neck and a square carton for a head. Large buttons form eyes and a wire coil serves as a nose. Notice the imaginative use of clothespins for legs. Grade six.**

Illus. 299. Here is Little Red Riding Hood on her way to her grandmother's house. Cardboard boxes are ideal for making dioramas. A great variety of materials have gone into this scene—from odd pieces of satin to twigs and leaves. Grade seven.

into interesting fragments. They can be laid down so that they overlap, or an equal space can be left between pieces and painted in later to suggest the grout or cement that is used in real mosaics.

Masonite, plywood, and corrugated cardboard all provide excellent backings for the applied materials. Milk-base glue serves as a satisfactory adhesive and a final coat of shellac prevents the tiny materials from flaking off.

## Carton Constructions

A supply of various cardboard cartons, including oatmeal boxes, dry cereal boxes, egg cartons, cardboard tubing, toothpaste boxes, gift boxes, and shoe boxes, can be assembled into either abstract or representational forms. Masking tape, staples and brass paper fasteners can be used to join the cartons together. Strips of newspaper, covered with white library paste, can be wrapped around the cartons to provide strength as well as a good painting surface. Many cartons have a waxy surface which makes painting difficult. This can be remedied by rubbing a paint-loaded brush on a bar of soap or a raw potato before applying it to the box.

A corrugated box provides a perfect material for a diorama. By removing one side, you have a stage setting which can be painted with tempera or decorated with paper. A cloth curtain can be hung on either side of the stage. (See Chapter Nine).

## Pop Bottle Figures

Illus. 301, believe it or not, has a pop-bottle body! This is a sixth-grader's conception of "Cinderella Dressed for the Ball." A pipe cleaner was inserted into a ball of cotton to make the head and a piece of nylon stocking was placed over the cotton ball and gathered at the base. A rubber band was used to hold the gathers taut and then the pipe cleaner was inserted into the mouth of the bottle.

**Illus. 300. A number of odd-sized cartons were cut, remodelled, and painted to form this attractive little train. Wooden spools are attached for wheels. Grade five.**

**Illus. 301. "Cinderella Dressed for the Ball."**
Would you have guessed this elegant lady
started out as a plain pop bottle?

Next, pipe cleaners, equalling a length of approximately 17 inches, were wound around the top part of the bottle. Two long ends were left protruding on either side to form the arms. Bits of crumpled toilet tissue were wound around the arms to plump them out. A long strip of toilet tissue, folded once in half, was wound around the bottle neck just below the arms to fill out the chest and shoulders. Then crepe paper was used to create the bodice, skirt and sleeves. Rickrack and sequins adorn the dress and paper ribbon provides golden locks. The elegant result certainly belies the ordinary pop-bottle base.

Any number of such figures, either imaginary or representational, can be formed in a similar fashion around bottles. You need not, of course, be restricted to pop bottles, but for representational figures their proportions are ideal. Tall wine bottles, rectangular milk bottles or juice bottles can also be used.

## Stabiles

Standing sculptural forms allow children to give vent to their construction ability as well as their esthetic sense. A ball of clay provides an excellent base into which sundry materials can be poked—pipe cleaners, twigs, etc. Delicate wire constructions can be made using a cork base or a cardboard base to which the wire is stapled.

Paper drinking straws are good materials to use for a stabile because a platform need not be used. The straws themselves provide "legs" for the structure as shown in Illus. 302. Starting from the bottom, each straw is attached to the next straw with straight pins and glue. When the glue is dry, the pins can be removed. Toothpicks, tongue depressors and reeds can be used too, but the smaller materials are best suited to the creative needs of older children. A project that is too difficult for a young child will defeat and frustrate him, so be sure to substitute materials that he can handle easily.

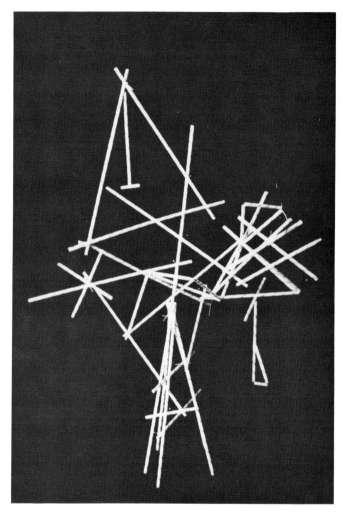

**Illus. 302.** Reed sculpture is particularly fascinating to older children such as the tenth-grade creator of this stabile. Reeds, straws, balsa wood, toothpicks can all be used. Here, drinking straws have been glued together to form a striking and delicately balanced stabile.

185

Illus. 303. This insect mobile was constructed by a fifth-grade class who used tissue paper, pipe cleaners, tinfoil, paper doilies, colored paper, and many other scrap materials. Each insect was hung from the ceiling lights with a single strand of thread.

Illus. 304. Two crossed pieces of wire form the basic frame for this mobile. Pieces of wire were shaped into ovals with twisted tails to suggest fish, covered with tissue paper, and suspended from the frame with crepe-paper strips.

## Mobiles

The possibilities for creating mobiles are enormous. Any number of materials and subjects can be made into mobiles. The scrap materials themselves will undoubtedly, as we said before, be the starting point for mobile construction. Our nonscientific insects shown in Illus. 303 through Illus. 307 are examples of this. The delicacy of colored tissue papers and colored pipe cleaners immediately conjured up imaginary and fanciful insects that would fill the air with color and movement when joined together.

The pipe cleaners are easily cut, joined or twisted into any form that imagination demands. If the insect is particularly large, a piece of strong wire can be added to give it support. The tissue paper can be easily attached to the wire frames with liquid starch or glue. You can

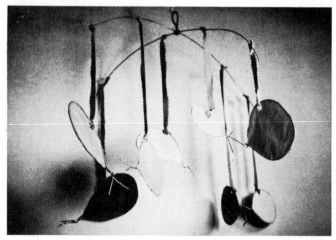

Illus. 305. This is one of the tissue-paper insects used in the mobile in Illus. 303. Sequins, ribbon, doilies, rickrack, pipe cleaners, all go together to form this graceful creature.

Illus. 306. Another of the insect members of the class mobile, but quite a different one! Tinfoil, shade pulls, cord, pipe cleaners and pieces of costume jewelry form an imaginative insect.

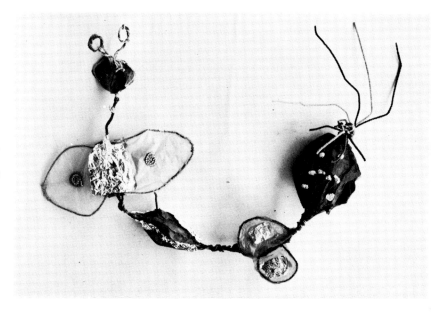

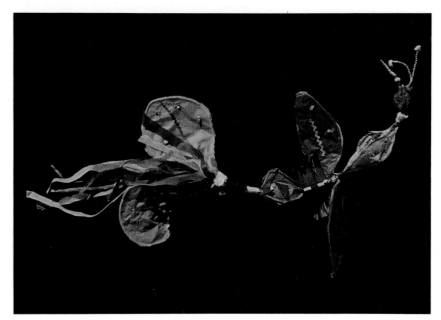

**Illus. 307. This beautiful tissue-paper insect is also part of the group in Illus. 303.**

obtain interesting effects by glueing different colored tissue together to form layers.

Wings, bodies, tails and antennae can be decorated with rickrack, tinfoil, button, glitter, paper doilies, yarn, sequins, lace, and bits of colored construction paper. When complete, hang the insects from ceiling lights by a single strand of thread or wire—the artificial lighting will intensify the luminous colors of the tissue and make the glitter and tinfoil sparkle.

If you have a collection of nuts, fruit, bits of shavings, drinking straws, table-tennis balls, or any variety of such objects, you can make fascinating mobiles. Scrap of all kinds never fails to provide a stimulating source for creative art and personal expression.

# THE AUTHOR

**Chester Jay Alkema**

Chester Jay Alkema was born and raised in the rural village of Martin, Michigan, and attended the Martin Agricultural High School. He graduated from Brandon High School, Brandon, Wisconsin, in 1950; received his A.B. degree in Education from Calvin College, Grand Rapids; earned his M.A. in Art in 1959 from Michigan State University, and his Masters of Fine Arts degree in 1961.

Prof. Alkema has taught art to children of the Seymour Christian School, Grand Rapids, Michigan, and the Wyoming Parkview School, Wyoming, Michigan, for many years. Since 1959, the author has taught adult art education courses for Michigan State University in East Lansing, Grand Rapids, Benton Harbor, Battle Creek and Niles. In the Spring of 1965, he joined the art faculty of Grand Valley State College, Allendale, Michigan.

Prof. Alkema has contributed numerous articles and photographs in the national educational journals, *Arts and Activities, School Arts, The Instructor, Grade Teacher, Design, Exceptional Children, Children's House,* and the foreign publication *Saber.* He has illustrated stories for *Crusader,* a magazine for children. This book, his fifth published by Sterling Publishing Co. since 1967, is the most recent addition to a hoped-for long list of published works.

# ACKNOWLEDGMENTS

The author extends special thanks to the children of Wyoming Parkview School, Wyoming, Michigan, and the Kalamazoo (Michigan) Public School children; also to the children of Allendale (Michigan) Public Schools; Grand Rapids (Michigan) Public Schools; Grandville (Michigan) Public Schools; to the classroom teachers, teachers' aides, practice teachers and students associated with Grand Valley State College and Michigan State University; to the publishers of *School Arts* for granting permission to use material and photographs from an article in the November, 1964, issue; to the publishers of *Arts and Activities* for granting permission to use material and photographs from articles in the October, 1963, and December, 1963, issues.

He would also like to thank the following for permission to photograph works of art which appear in this book: Mr. Joseph Brozak, Assistant Superintendent of the Wyoming Public Schools; Mr. Donald O. Martz, Principal of the Wyoming Public Schools; Dr. Richard N. Percy, Superintendent of the Kalamazoo (Michigan) Public Schools; Miss Marian Andros, Supervisor of Art, Kalamazoo (Michigan) Public Schools; Mrs. James Boyce III, Saugatuck, Michigan; Sherwood Park Elementary School, Grand Rapids, Michigan; Northview High School, Grand Rapids, Michigan; Mona Shores High School, Muskegon, Michigan; The American Crayon Company; Joanne Quint, teacher, Oakleigh Elementary School, Grand Rapids, Michigan; Arlene Scripsema, teacher, Grandville (Michigan) Public Schools; Mrs. Jeannette Ben-Attar, nursery-school teacher; and Mrs. Paul Hines, nursery-school teacher.

The author would also like to thank the following people for supplying photographs which appear in this book: Mr. John F. Agee, Los Alamos, New Mexico; Mrs. Kate Keffer Agee, Art Chairman, Los Alamos (New Mexico) Public Schools; *Grand Rapids Press*, Michigan; Mr. Joseph Greco, art teacher, Godwin Public Schools, Wyoming, Michigan; Binney & Smith, Inc.; Edith Brockway; and Don Chrysler, Principal of the Central Elementary School, Grandville, Michigan.

# Index